Criminal Justice

In the United States

Criminal Justice

In the United States

by

Rick Becker

First Edition: January 2018
Printed in the United States of America
Front cover design: Rick Becker
ISBN: 978-0-359-27180-1

To my children, you are my life.

Table of Contents

About the Author

Rick Becker is a Father of six, husband, and a Security Specialist who was born in Long Island, New York. Rick currently resides just outside of Indianapolis, Indiana.

Within the course of three years, he proudly served in the United States Army Infantry. He was also a passionate Team Leader for MND North Quick Reaction Force, in Operation Joint Forge, during the Kosovo Crisis. He currently serves as a Military Police officer, for the Indiana Guard Reserve, where he has been serving for the last two years.

Throughout the years, Rick has been infinitely dedicated to his field and received numerous awards, including the Army Commendation Medal, Army Achievement Medal, Armed Forces Expeditionary Medal, Armed Forces Service Medal, Humanitarian Service Medal, Army Service Ribbon, NATO Medal, IGR Physical Fitness Ribbon, IGR CERT Ribbon, IGR Emergency Management Specialist Ribbon Indiana Defense Service Ribbon and the Expert Rifle Marksmanship Badge.

Additionally, Rick has received in-depth training via the Federal Government, as a civilian employee. He possesses over twenty-two certifications, primarily through the Department of Homeland Security. These various accreditations include

Leadership and Influence, Decision Making and Problem Solving, Technical Writing, Emergency Planning, State Disaster Management, HazMat for Medical Personnel, Developing and Managing Volunteers, Introduction to Hazmat, Radiological Emergency Response, Effective Communication, Intro to CERT, Active Shooter and Preparing for Mass Casualty Incidents: Guide for Schools, Higher Education, and Houses of Worship.

Knowing no limitations, Rick has even successfully completed numerous certification courses through Columbia University and the National Center for Disaster Preparedness. Among these accreditations: Fundamentals of Emergency Preparedness, Elements of Leadership: Decision-Making and Problem-Solving Under Emergency Conditions, Dealing with Disaster-Related Trauma in Children, and Chemical Terrorism Laboratory Level 3 Training for Hospitals: Clinical Specimen Collection and Handling. And finally, he holds a Certification for Surveillance Law from Stanford University.

Furthermore, Rick obtained his bachelor's degree in Criminal Justice with a minor in Forensic Psychology, graduating Summa cum Laude. During his time at university, he was a member of a multitude of National Honor Societies. Currently, Rick is continuing his education at Purdue University and is meticulously working towards his Master of Science in Communications graduate degree.

Introduction

The three main components of the Criminal Justice System are police, courts, and corrections. The duty of a police officer is to enforce laws and make arrests. There is a misconception that police have a duty to “serve and protect”, this is a fallacy. According to a Supreme Court Ruling, Police have no Constitutional duty to protect anyone, unless the individual is in Police Custody. "The Supreme Court ruled on Monday that the police did not have a constitutional duty to protect a person from harm, even a woman who had obtained a court-issued protective order against a violent husband making an arrest mandatory for a violation." (Greenhouse, 2005).

The next component is the courts. Courts make decisions on whether there is enough evidence for a defendant to be tried for a crime, the courts also make decisions in sentencing. The prosecutor must first write an information, before the Courts decide if they will even take the case. "In some states, the prosecutor may seek to continue the case against a defendant by filing an information with the court. An information, which is a formal written accusation, is filed on the basis of the outcome of the preliminary hearing." (Schmalleger, 2015, p.

18).

The third component is corrections. Corrections is the final step for a convicted criminal. Corrections is where a criminal serves jail or prison time. "Some offenders are sentenced to prison, where they “do time” for their crimes. Once in the correctional system, they are classified according to local procedures and are assigned to confinement facilities and treatment programs." (Schmalleger, 2015, p. 20).

There is no part of the system that is worse, or better than any other part of the system. According to the Consensus model of criminal justice, "each of the component parts of the criminal justice system strives toward a common goal that a movement of cases and people through the system is smooth due to cooperation between the various components of the system." (Schmalleger, 2015, p. 13).

It is the duty of each component of the system to be fair and balanced and follow procedural and Constitutional Laws. Out of the three components of the Criminal Justice System, there is not one individual part that could be "most harmful". It potentially, would not be possible for one part of the system to be more harmful than another.

Regarding Police, there are many instances where people believe police violated their rights. This is also true of the court, and corrections as well. In courts, there are many wrongful convictions. There are also many times where you read newspaper articles about prisoners being abused, or mistreated.

Although the system is set up to be fair and balanced, the system still contains human elements. If there are human elements, there is potential for misuse, and abuse of power, equally in all three components. These instances of injustice are few and far between. Overall, the criminal justice system does work as a whole. There is not any part of the system that is worse, or better than any other part. Belief in the system is why the Criminal Justice system is fair. It should be believed that every person, that is a part of the system, feels that same core belief.

Chapter 1

Terrorism

TERRORISM DEFINED

Terrorism is classified as a crime in the United States of America today. For a person to be charged with terrorism, there must be a universal definition for terrorism. Is there a different interpretation, or meaning behind the word terrorism from a sociological approach, versus a legal approach?

The term terrorism was first coined approximately 1,900 years ago. "The root of the word terrorism is taken from a Latin term that means "to frighten". It became part of the phrase *terror cimbricus*, which was used by ancient Romans in 105BC to describe the panic that ensued as they prepared for an attack by a fierce warrior tribe." (Crime Museum LLC, 2015). From its origins, the word terrorism was identified as fear related to an attack.

In more modern times, the evolution of the word terrorism has changed. The terrorist has also evolved with time as well. This may have a relation, or this may just be part of the natural progression of society. "Nobody has been able to produce an exact definition. As a result, *terrorism* means different things to different people." (White, 2011, p. 4). From a societal standpoint, the word terrorism may have different meanings. Terrorism may also have a different meaning depending on where a person lives geographically. This can be proven by the widely used phrase first written by Gerald Seymour, in his 1975 Book, "One man's terrorist is another man's freedom fighter". (Seymour, 1975). The phrase was later made popular in the United States from a 1986 Ronald Reagan radio address.

The next definition of the word terrorism is more detrimental than what society perceives the definition to be. The definition that could be interpreted as being more fundamentally important, is the legal definition of the word terrorism. “For the sake of developing and evaluating public policy decisions aimed at combating **terrorism**, we need a precise public **definition** of **terrorism** that distinguishes **terrorism** from other forms of violence.” (Reitan, 2010). The Federal Bureau of Investigation also has their own definition of the word terrorism. According to 18 U.S.C. § 2331, terrorism can be broken down into two types of terrorism. These two types of terrorism are domestic terrorism, and international terrorism.

Each one of these forms of terrorism consists of three parts, according to the FBI’s definition of terrorism. For a crime to legally considered terrorism by FBI standards, for both domestic, and international terrorism, the crime must; “Involve violent acts or acts dangerous to human life that violate federal or state law”, and “Appear to be intended (i) to intimidate or coerce a civilian population; (ii) to influence the policy of a government by intimidation or coercion; or (iii) to affect the conduct of a government by mass destruction, assassination, or kidnapping" (18 U.S.C. § 2331).

The last part of the legal definition varies, this depends on if the crime of terrorism is domestic, or international. For the third part of the legal definition of terrorism, according to the FBI legal standard, both domestic, and international terrorism must also; "Occur primarily within the territorial jurisdiction of the U.S." (18 U.S.C. § 2331). For the crime to be considered international terrorism, the U.S. legal code definition continues to read "or transcend national boundaries in terms of the means by which they are accomplished, the persons they appear intended to intimidate or coerce, or the locale in which their perpetrators operate or seek asylum. (18 U.S.C. § 2331).

There are many definitions of what terrorism may be. The three basic differences in these definitions are if the definition comes from a societal, geographical or a legal interpretation of the word. Depending on who is interpreting the word, you may always get more than one interpretation of the term terrorism.

TERROSTIC CRIME VS CRIME

Terroristic crime and many common crimes have a similar structure. The main differences between common crime and terrorism is the motivation behind the crime, or the criminal act. "When a crime is politically motivated, the commission says it is terrorism. The problem with this approach is that a crime is a crime no matter what motivation lies behind the action. Except in times of conflict or governmental repression, all terrorism involves criminal activity." (White, 2011). Again, Terrorism is considered a crime in the United States of America today. For a person to be charged with terrorism, there must be a universal definition for terrorism. Is there a different interpretation, or meaning behind the word terrorism from a sociological approach, and a legal approach?

Motivation behind terrorism:

- Political Motivation
- Religious Motivation
- Economic Factors
- Ethnic Factors
- Social Factors

The motivation that lies behind a terroristic criminal act stem from the criminal, or terrorist, committing the crime for a group cause. The crime, or terroristic act, is justified to the terrorist by the ideology of thoughts that are shared by the group. Some people would arguably state that Economic Factors have no basis as far as the motivation behind terrorist attack. The statements made go as far as declaring "most of the people who sacrificed their lives for the sake of Allah were engineers and had office jobs." (Al-Yazji, 2014)

Motivation of crimes:

- Racially Motivated
- Self Interest
- Environmental
- Opportunity
- Association to other criminals
- Labeling
- Biology

There are many theories as to the reasons why people commit crimes. Some crimes are racially motivated, which in itself is a crime of self-interest, or could be in relation to the environment a person grew up in. These motivations can be broken down into; "Rational Choice Theory, Social Disorganization Theory, Strain Theory, Social Learning Theory, Social Control Theory, Labeling Theory, Biology, Labeling and Genetics" (Lanier/ Briggs, et. al, 2014). These theories are all forms of the study of Criminology.

Religious Terrorists:

1. Reject the modern world
2. Refuse to accept secular society
3. View the world as evil
4. Violence occurs when sacred traditions are threatened.
5. Requires some to make "sacrifices"

Scholars feel as though organizations like Al-

Qaeda are more focused on the martyrdom aspect of the terrorism, making the religious aspect the most important part of the actual terrorist act. This type of behavior has been demonstrated by the Mujahedeen since the Afghan war with the Soviet Union. Mujahedeen's fighters in the former Yugoslavia, and the more modern Iraqi, and Afghanistan wars were motivated by similar martyrdom motivations.

Political Terrorists:

1. Part of a social process
2. Usually has religious motivation
3. Consists of violent actions

Experts feel that most terrorism, although done for political gain, is based off of religious context. Terrorist organizations use religion to motivate terrorists to commit the acts of terrorism. "It has embraced many modern nationalistic movements, and militant religious imagery is used to reinforce mainstream political concepts." (White, 2011).

Cultural aspects of Crime:

"People who engage in criminal behavior, do so within the context of subcultural and cultural contexts that inform cognitive scripts and schema—what kind of music, clothing, weapons, language, mannerisms, accessories, and so on are associated with what kind of people, places and behaviors." (Helfgott, 2008, p. 78)

Most researches would agree that the cultural

aspects of crime, all stem from subcultures of crime. Many sub cultures of crime can be related to the music, dress, and group thinking of the congregate, or sub-congregates that the criminals associate with. This subculture also helps shape how these criminals choose their victims.

Cultural aspects of Terrorism:

Defined by:

1. Economic Systems
2. Social Structures
3. Behaviors
4. Values
5. Religion

The cultural aspects of terrorism are believed to stem from "The Clash of Civilization". Huntington believes that these clashes, that may cause terrorism, are rooted in the clash between the world's eight dominant civilizations. "Civilizations are defined by common mores, values, behaviors, social structures, and economic systems. Religion is a key factor in defining a civilization." (White, 2011)

Historical Perspectives

Terrorism itself has not changed much throughout history. The motivation behind terrorism itself also has historically carried a political motivation. The main changes in how terrorism is perceived, or how terroristic acts are committed, has changed little, and mainly through definition.

"One common misconception is that terrorism is a new and unprecedented phenomenon. In actuality, terrorism is not an invention of modern times." (Digital History, 2014). When studying terrorism, there are three perspectives. The first of these principles is the psychological principle. "Social psychologists describe one's environment as the place where a person's behaviour is influenced by the social settings in which they live and their psychological predispositions." (de la Corte, 2007). This psychological perspective hypothesizes that terrorism is influenced by the environment in which individuals are raised in. Similar to some societal criminological perspectives.

The second perspective is that terrorism is shaped off of social interactions, or the social circles in which whom individuals associate with. "Previously, some researchers suggested that the process of joining a terrorist group was heavily influenced by the prevailing political and social environment shared by friends and relatives." (de la Corte, 2007). This perspective presents the idea that individuals are influenced to join terrorist organizations or commit terrorist acts based off influence from their social circle.

The third perspective of understanding terrorism is that terrorists are linked to social movements. "Very often, terrorist campaigns are the result of a long radicalization process of certain political or religious movement. When those movements lose their social influence, they tend to split off and form different groups." (de la Corte, 2007). With this third principle, researchers hold the belief that terrorism is committed as part of a social, or political movement. The motivation behind the crime is to fulfill a political, or social agenda.

Since the first terrorist attacks in history, not much has changed, as far as the motivation behind terrorist acts. Many of these terrorist organizations use religion to gain support for their organizations. One example of this is the 1917 bombing in Milwaukee, Wisconsin. This attack was done by anarchists and resulted in the death of nine police officers. The attack was committed to fulfill their political motivation behind the group's anarchist movement. Another example is a nationwide bombing campaign that took place in June of 1919, also organized by anarchists in the United States. Anarchists set off a string of eight bombs, in eight cities. This attack resulted in the death of 40, and an injury count of over 300 individuals. Again, these attacks were to reinforce the beliefs of the anarchist party, to spread fear, and deliver a political message.

Finally, the September 11th, 2001 attacks against the United States. This attack was organized by Al-Qaeda. The attack consisted of a group of well-educated individuals, who were part of a terrorist organization, using planes as missiles and attacking civilian targets. These attacks resulted in the loss of thousands of lives. These attacks took place almost 100 years after the attacks by the anarchists, but again maintained a similar theme.

The historical perspective on terrorism has not

changed, particularly in the United States. The biggest changes that have been made, historically, are the way in which we now deal with terroristic attacks. Many new laws, and task forces have been enacted to protect United States citizens from terror attacks. This, historically, is the biggest impact terrorism has had on our Country, and the world.

FUNDING TERRORISM

One of the main factors of stopping terrorism, is stopping the funding of individual terrorist organizations. Funding for a terrorist organization can be a force multiplier. To help eliminate terrorism, we must identify where terrorist funding is coming from. "Terrorist groups are increasingly turning to alternative sources of financing, including criminal activities such as arms trafficking, money laundering, kidnap-for-ransom, extortion, racketeering, and drug trafficking." (Financial Action Task Force, 2008, p. 34). Charities, money laundering, and drug trafficking are three major sources of funding for terrorist organizations.

Charities are a big source of funding for most terroristic organizations. "Terrorist organizations often exploit the principle of *zakat*, or charity-one of the five pillars of Islam. (Baradaran/Findley, et. al, 2014, p. 490). Using charities to funnel money to support terrorism is also beneficial to terrorist organizations, as non-profit organizations are not highly regulated. Al-Qaeda was famously funded through donations from donors. "Among the sources of *Al-Qaeda*'s income we find since its inception funds diverted from charitable organisations, profits gained from businesses run by its members and sympathisers and money collected by fundraisers seeking donations." (del Cid Gómez, 2010).

Money laundering is also one of the largest, if not the largest, money maker for terrorist organizations. The United States Department of Treasury has created a department to help prevent money laundering in terrorist organizations. They are referred to as the Office of Terrorism and Financial Intelligence, or TFI. The goal of the United States Department of Treasury is "combating all aspects of money laundering at home and abroad, through the mission of the Office of Terrorism and Financial Intelligence (TFI)." (U.S. Dept. of Treasury, 2015). Money laundering is common practice, and terrorists often use electronic purchasing systems to launder money into their organization.

Drug trafficking is also a vital source of funding for terrorist organizations. It is commonly known that "various terrorist groups derive significant financial benefit from other criminal activities, including through drug trafficking." (U.S. Dept. of Treasury, 2015, p. 16). Drug trafficking is efficient for terrorist organizations, as they can raise money within their own networks. "According to Spanish police informants, drugs trafficking groups operating in the North African enclaves Ceuta and Melilla send a portion of the profits from hashish trafficking to finance Islamic terrorist groups, with whose cause they sympathise." (del Cid Gómez, 2010).

There are many financial sources that terrorist organizations use to raise funds. Most of these sources are of an illegal nature. It can be seen, however, that terrorist organizations are also receiving funds from legitimate businesses as well. Funding terrorist organizations is a global business, and it is going to take a global effort to stop terrorist funding.

THE INTERNET AND TERRORISM

Terrorists, and the term terrorism have been present in society since the late 1700's. The principles of terrorism have remained the same. Another one of the main changes in terrorism, has been the implementation of modern technology by terrorists, and terrorist organizations. One of the key pieces of technology for terrorists, and terrorist organizations, most recently, is the internet.

The theory of the internet was first discussed by a DARPA researcher in 1962. It was not until three years later that "in 1965 working with Thomas Merrill, Roberts connected the TX-2 computer in Mass. to the Q-32 in California with a low speed dial-up telephone line creating the first (however small) wide-area computer network ever built." (Leiner/Serf, et. al, 1995). This experiment proved that the internet was possible. The internet has since evolved into technology that we now refer to as the world-wide web.

It is through the technology of the modern-day internet, that the current terrorist networks are emerging. “Today, all active terrorist groups have established their presence on the Internet” (Weimann, 2004). Terrorist organizations use the internet, due to its convenience, the anonymity factor, and the ability to quickly disseminate information.

Terrorist organizations are known to use the internet in many ways. The first of these functions is for psychological warfare. The terrorist group ISIS, which is headed by Abu Bakr al-Baghdadi, is the most recently publicized of the terrorist organizations to instill fear, implementing psychological operation like tactics. The terrorist group ISIS has most recently uploaded videos on the internet of their members beheading victims, burning victims alive, and drowning victims in cages.

ISIS, which stands for, Islamic State of Iraq and Syria, is a splinter group of al-Qaeda. ISIS is believed to have been founded in 2006, in Iraq. ISIS believes that they are “to create an Islamic state, referred to as a caliphate, across Iraq, Syria and beyond.” (CNN Library, 2017). The internet is one tool that ISIS is using to spread their message, and to recruit new followers and members.

There has yet to be much action taken against ISIS by any Countries to this date. Allies within the United Nations have started bombing campaigns, to help destroy persons of interest, within the ISIS network. Even with the tactics that ISIS is using, attacking innocent civilians, President Barrack Obama, or any other allied countries of the Unites States of America have yet to launch an all-out offensive attack against ISIS fighters in the Middle East.

Within the United States, there have been arrests in relation to individuals who have provided support to ISIS. Other than this minimal response, ISIS continues to violate International law, terrorize citizens, and kill innocent civilians. There is no doubt, that the modern technology of the internet is helping ISIS spread the word about their organizations to potential supporters. It is through this technology that this organization is growing and becoming stronger. Some may feel the President of the United States sits by idly watching, as ISIS uses the internet to make itself stronger, and spread their message to the world.

Summary of Domestic Terrorism in the U.S.

Domestic terrorism in the United States is a homegrown problem within the United States. Domestic terrorists differ from foreign terrorists in the fact that they are comprised of a very diverse spectrum of hate groups. "One difference between jihadist-type terrorism and domestic terrorism is that jihadists are always in a slow-boil," making them a steady threat to the U.S., he said, "whereas domestic extremists tend to be more reactive. They aren't always as inclined to just lash out without a situation." (Berger, 2014). The Southern Poverty Law center lists over 60 Domestic terrorist attacks in the United States since the Oklahoma City bombing.

The Department of Homeland Security was not thought of until after the attacks against the World Trade Center in NY on 9/11. It was because of the attacks on 9/11 that the nation felt they needed to take a better, more organized stand to fight terrorism. In June 2002 President George W. Bush proposed the creation of The Department of Homeland Security. George W. Bush Stated, ""The President proposes to create a new Department of Homeland Security, the most significant transformation of the U.S. government in over half-century by largely transforming and realigning the current confusing patchwork of government activities into a single department whose primary mission is to protect our homeland. The creation of a Department of Homeland Security is one more key step in the President's national strategy for homeland security." (Bush, 2002).

On July 23rd, 2002 The Homeland Security Act of 2002 was put into legislation. This 187-page document was an integral part in the creation of what is now known as the Department of Homeland Security. Within this act, The Department of Homeland Security was deemed to be an Executive Department of the United States Government. **Many agencies are part of The Department of Homeland Security, today these agencies are**

known as:

1. U.S. Customs and Border Protection
2. U.S. Immigration and Customs Enforcement
3. U.S. Citizenship and Immigration Services
4. Transportation Security Administration
5. Federal Law Enforcement Training Center
6. Federal Emergency Management Agency
7. U.S. Coast Guard
8. U.S. Secret Service
9. U.S. Cert
10. Science and Technology Directorate
11. Office of Cybersecurity and Communications

Left-wing Terrorist Groups:

- ***Puerto Rican National Liberation-*** carried out bombings on the U.S. mainland, primarily in and around New York City. (1970's-1980's)
- ***Los Macheteros-*** March 31, 1998 bombing of a superaquaduct project in Arecibo, the bombings of bank offices in Rio Piedras and Santa Isabel in June 1998, and the bombing of a highway in Hato Rey in 1999.
- ***Animal Liberation Front/ Earth Liberation Front-*** The FBI estimates that ALF/ELF have committed approximately 600 criminal acts in the United States since 1996, resulting in damages in excess of 42 million dollars

Source- *(FBI.gov, 2002)*

Philosophy of Left-wing groups- Lenin/Marxist philosophy to overthrow the current government structure and put a socialist Government in place.

Right-wing Terrorist Groups:

- ***Oklahoma Constitutional Militia*** - prepared explosives to bomb numerous targets, including the Southern Poverty Law Center, gay bars and abortion clinics.
- ***Silent Brotherhood*** - carried out assassinations and armored car heists.
- ***North American Militia of Southwestern Michigan*** - conspired to bomb federal buildings, a Kalamazoo television station and an interstate highway interchange, kill federal agents, assassinate politicians and attack aircraft at a National Guard base — attacks that were all to be funded by marijuana sales.

Source- *(SPLC, 2012)*

Philosophy of right-wing groups - a political philosophy that resists any change in the existing political, economic, social and religious institutions and beliefs. It aims to protect traditional values and beliefs, mainly religious, from the perceived threats of the 'others'." (Ahmed, 2015).

Foreign-born Terrorist Groups:

Foreign born terrorist groups differ from right wing, or left wing domestic terrorist groups in the United States. One of the main differences is the fact that right and left-wing terrorist groups are mostly citizens who are born here in the United States.

One of the main threats in the United States when it comes to Foreign-born terrorist groups is the lack of security at the United States Borders. In 2005, Janice Gephart Said, "a study of the activities of ninety-four foreign-born terrorists who operated in the United States from 1990 to 2004 shows the inadequacy of enforcement. Two-thirds of the terrorists engaged in criminal activities before or in conjunction with their terrorist attacks." (White, 2011, p. 519).

It became apparent after the 9/11 attacks that foreign born terrorist, from the like of Al-Qaida were capable of committing effective attacks on U.S. Soil. Most of Foreign-Born Terrorist groups that attack the United States are motivated by one philosophy. Jihad is the main philosophy, or inspiration behind their attacks. The wish to wage a holy war against the United States, and all infidels.

Challenges to Homeland Security:

1. The United States can-not use the military to combat domestic terrorism, so they must rely upon the militarization of law enforcement agencies.
2. Domestic terrorists are afforded certain Civil Rights as American Citizens that foreign-born terrorists are not entitled to. "Under the Fourth Amendment, law enforcement personnel cannot collect intelligence without the standard of reasonable suspicion."

(White, 2011, p. 558)

3. The Sharing of intelligence between agencies. "The 9/11 Commission Report (2004, pp. 339-348) criticizes federal agencies for failing to recognize and share intelligence." (White, 2011, p. 556).
4. Border enforcement, and protection. "Terrorists enter the United States with temporary visas and then fail to follow the provisions of entry. They make false statements on applications and lie on other official documents while in the country. They make sham marriages or utilize other loopholes to stay in the country." (White, 2011, p. 519).
5. The gathering of intelligence by local law enforcement officials. "The process of gathering defense intelligence is not readily apparent in American policing. Most law enforcement officers did not enter police ranks thinking that they were joining an army or aspiring to be part of DHS." (White, 2011, p. 523)

Ethics

In the legal system, many investigators, attorneys and judges are faced with ethical issues. When dealing with terrorism there are many ethical issues to consider. Some ethical issues are dealt with mainly by investigators alone, while other ethical and moral issues are to be dealt with by prosecutors and judges. Regardless of your position in the legal system, making moral and ethical decisions is integral, and “it is essential that counterterrorism professionals are proficient at making these types of decision.” (Reding/Walczak, et. al, 2014, p. 15)

When it comes to the ethics of prosecuting terror suspects, there are many gray areas. The topic of ethics itself, is not such a black and white issue. One of the main issues with dealing with terrorists as a crime is determining where, and how to try terror suspects in court. The main issue is that of a jurisdictional issue. Since terrorists are technically considered enemy combatants, should terrorism be tried as a criminal offense, or as an act of war against our military?

To address this issue, the first thing that must be decided is what legal system contains, or has, jurisdiction to detain and try a terror suspect. Some people believe that jurisdiction belongs to the military, a “defence authorisation bill that funds the US military, effectively extends the battlefield in the "war on terror" to the US and applies the established principle that combatants in any war are subject to military detention.” (McGreal, 2011). Others believe that terror suspects have equal rights and deserve the right to be tried in Federal Courts and be given proper Due Process procedural rights. To be able to try any suspect, one side will decide who gets to effectively take custody of the suspect. This decision alone has a large impact on the rights of the accused in court.

Under the assumption that a suspect is detained

by the military, as an enemy combatant, that suspect no longer is entitled to due process rights. The manner in which the evidence is collected is not imperative to the detainment of said suspect. “The law applies to anyone "who was a part of or substantially supported al-Qaida, the Taliban or associated forces". (McGreal, 2011). Essentially, it must be determined if the terror suspect is related to any of these intertwined terrorist organizations, before trying the accused in court. It could be argued that these suspects are being denied the right to a fair and speedy trial.

If the suspect is not a part of one of these terrorist organizations, and they are part of a more single-issue group, then due process procedures prevail. For example, if the suspect is part of an animal rights organization, “sometimes progress to criminal activities.” (Osterburg/Ward, 2014). Under these circumstance, a suspect’s due process rights must be adhered to. All evidence must be obtained according to proper procedure. Any evidence that a judge considers admissible must be obtained through proper legal channels. It may be presumptuous to consider proper legal channels as ethical, but these legal channels are the most ethical avenues that we as a people have decided upon.

In the situations where a terrorism suspect is tried outside of the military court system, investigators must have taken ethical, and proper procedural steps to obtain any evidence against the suspect. If any, or a majority of the evidence was not obtained using the avenues of, pen trap warrants, search warrants, and probable cause procedures, the charges may even be dropped before going to court. If it was found out that this evidence was obtained in an immoral fashion during the court proceedings, it is possible there can be a mistrial, or specific piece of evidence may be omitted under the exclusionary rule.

It is probable to speculate that the most caution to ethical, and moral procedure need be taken in the proactive approach of investigating terrorism. Due to the fact that the proactive approach is a preventative measure of investigating terrorism, more proper procedures for obtaining the evidence must be followed. When being proactive during an investigation, and investigator may need to tap a phone line, or install listening devices. It would be absolutely imperative to the case, in court, for the investigator to obtain a warrant when gathering this type of information.

In a reactive approach to investigating terrorism, there is the same need of importance to follow ethical and legal procedures, however, with the reactive approach, the crime has already been committed. Essentially, the investigators are obtaining evidence by recreating the crime. In a reactive approach, a majority of the evidence may come from the crime scene itself. Bomb fragments may be put back together, or video footage may be sorted through. There would also be many witness interviews that needed to take place, in order to obtain information about the crime. A good majority of these investigative procedures do not require warrants. If warrants are not obtained in the gathering of the evidence in both reactive, and proactive policing, the suspect's rights to unlawful search and seizure may be violated. Therefore, the state would not be able to prosecute.

When doing any investigation, including terrorism investigations, it is important for law enforcement to be both ethical, and moral when conducting the investigation. The best way for an investigator to do this, is to follow procedure of the Department, and follow procedural law pertaining to warrants, and the collection of evidence. Regardless of where the investigators believe the crime will be tried, in a military court, or a civilian court, it is safest for all of us as a society if the investigators follow the ethical, and lawful procedures put in place to get more potentially violent terrorists off American soil.

Chapter 2

Corrections

THE UNITED STATES CORRECTIONAL SYSTEM

The United States Correctional System is for punishment and rehabilitation of criminal offenders who are convicted of crimes. When we think of Corrections, the first thought that might come to our mind is punishment in prison, or jail for a crime. The correctional system is set up for both punishment and rehabilitation of criminal offenders. The Correctional system deals with criminal offenders through both punishment, and rehabilitation services.

When the word punishment is used in reference to criminal offenders, this is usually referring to a sentence of time in prison. Prior to the Constitution in the United States, and in other Countries, the term punishment may have had a more archaic implication. These punishments may have been some sort of torture. The Eighth Amendment in the United States Constitution states, "Excessive bail shall not be required, nor excessive fines imposed, nor cruel and unusual punishment inflicted" (U.S. Const., amendment VIII). It is because of the United States Constitution that the word punishment is referring more towards prison. "The use of prisons as places where convicted offenders serve time as PUNISHMENT for breaking the law is a relatively new development in the handling of offenders" (Schmalleger, 2014, p. 414).

Rehabilitation is also a part of the United States correctional system. Rehabilitation is an integral part of the re-integration of criminals back into society. Rehabilitation should be considered the most important part of the United States correctional system. Simply locking an offender up and punishing the offender for their crimes, does not prepare an offender to re-enter society, and may cause more repeat offenses. With rehabilitation, offenders are often offered skills, and education to help improve their mental well-being.

California has a program specifically designed to help rehabilitate offenders during their incarceration. According to the Department of Rehabilitative Programs website, they offer offenders programs such as: Substance abuse, high school diploma, and parole work crew programs (California Department of Corrections and Rehabilitative Services, 2015). Each State has their own specific rehabilitative programs for incarcerated offenders, and some programs are available on the Federal level as well.

Rehabilitation is a more effective approach in lowering the recidivism rate of repeat offenders. For non-violent offenders, probation used in conjunction with pre-trial diversion programs has an extremely high rate of non-repeat criminal offenders. According to a study from Kentucky's Pretrial Services Agency, listed on the American Bar Association's website, non-violent offenders with misdemeanors benefit greatly from rehabilitation services such as pretrial diversion programs. "In 2008, the PSA actively monitored 3,668 diversion clients with a success rate of 71% for its general misdemeanor diversion programs." (American Bar Association, 2015).

In the case of violent offenders, non-community-based rehabilitation services such as prison based rehabilitative programs are a more appropriate sentence. For violent offenders, giving them educational tools for success is pertinent to their success upon release into the community. It is necessary for violent offenders to be punished, as well as rehabilitated, with both parts being equally important. Without an education or behavioral health services, a violent offender who is released back into civilization may resort back to crime in desperation.

If a violent offender who is sentenced to prison does their time, and is a model prisoner, the offender may be offered parole. Parole is a form of community-based rehabilitation. "Probation is a sentencing strategy, but parole is a corrections strategy whose primary purpose is to return offenders gradually to productive lives. By making early release possible, parole can also act as a stimulus for positive behavioral change." (Schmalleger, 2014, p. 388). Parole implemented with programs such as the parole work crew program, will most likely have an overall positive effect on an offender's mental state. The offender also has a chance to work with members of the community in their rehabilitation, while finishing out their sentence.

In the United States Correctional System, the nature of the crime has direct correlation in the effectiveness of punishment versus rehabilitative services. In both offenders who commit violent, and non-violent crimes, rehabilitative services should still be implemented to help lower recidivism rates. The main determination of which type of program should be implemented, depends upon the seriousness of the crime. It should be noted, however, that rehabilitative services have a positive effect on most offenders regardless of the crime.

SOCIETAL VIEW ON CRIME

Society and their view of crime and punishment has evolved since the inception of crime and punishment was implemented. In its early days, punishment was the most accepted form of retribution for crimes. In modern times, within the last 100 years, society's view has evolved. The United States has shown the most evolution since the early 1800's.

Prior to any corrections systems in the United States, European Countries had their own form of punishment for crime. In the 1700's England was known for being one of the cruelest, or harsh prison systems to exist. "The worst felons were cut off from all contact with other prisoners; they had no hope of pardon to relieve their solitude or isolation. They were forced to remain alone and silent during the entire day, and breaking rules resulted in brutal punishments." (Seigel, 2011, p. 14). The ramifications of these types of punishments lead to wide spread mental breakdowns, suicides, and self-mutilation of prisoners in the system. These types of behaviors lead society to believe that England needed prison reform.

During the same time-period, Australia was going through a similar situation. This time-period brought about many reforms in the system. The 1700's time-period, could be considered the birth of indeterminate sentencing. Walter Crofton was one of the first prison reformers to gain International notoriety from a system he developed to help reform prisoners, and prisons. In Crofton's system, prisoners would work towards goals to be released early. These goals were set up in a step system. "Crofton believed in reformation, and inmates could earn early release or "tickets-of-leave" if they demonstrated achievement and positive attitude change." (Seigel, 2011, p. 15).

In the United States, the first penitentiaries were started in the Pennsylvania Quaker System, under the supervision of William Penn. The theory was that prisoners would go to penitentiaries for penance. These sentences were flat sentences that would be considered determinate sentences by today's standards. There was no exception for good behavior, and there was no possibility of early release. "Penitents entered penitentiaries to reform themselves during a pre-arranged length of stay (a flat sentence). At the end of their time, they were released under an assumption of repentance but without any formal assessment." (Chambliss, 2011, p. 62). So initially penitentiaries were set up in the United States as a form of penance for sinners.

In the early 1800's as well, New York state started to implement its own system of punishment for crime. New York began to implement what was called "good time laws". These laws allowed prisoners who were incarcerated to earn time for good behavior. This time would reduce the length of the prisoner's sentences. "By the mid-1800s, nearly half the states had good-time laws in place. Abroad, Captain Alexander Maconochie, the Scottish Warden of Norfolk Island—a notoriously rough Australian prison—developed the mark system, where inmates could earn their freedom early through hard work and good behavior." (Chambliss, 2011, p. 62).

In more modern times, society has also recognized the need for rehabilitation through corrections. This need has been mostly recognized for non-violent offenders in the form of Community Corrections. Community corrections consists of programs such as Diversion programs, probation, and even parole. With diversion programs, convicts are given a chance to enter a program, pre-trial, and complete the program in order to have their sentences reduced or erased from their records.

Probation is also a form of community corrections. "Following its beginnings as a voluntary movement in the late nineteenth century, probation experienced rapid growth in the first decades of the twentieth century and in the 1960s." (Seigel, 2011, p. 59). The rapid increase in probation is used as a means to help lessen the caseload of the prison system. With probation, offenders are allowed to live in the community, where the offenders are monitored by probation officer. The offenders are forced to follow stipulations such as living drug free, attending diversion programs, or community service to name a few.

The overall consensus in society, for mostly non-violent offenders, is to allow the convicted to rehabilitate themselves. Punishment seems to be more accepted for violent offenders, as punishment is deemed to be crueler on offenders than rehabilitation in general. The focus on community corrections in society in the United States at the current time, draws the conclusion that society is more focused on rehabilitating offender, than punishing offenders.

DETERMINATE VS. INDETERMINATE SENTENCING

Indeterminate, and determinate sentencing are two types of sentencing that are opposite on the spectrum when it comes to sentencing. Indeterminate sentencing has been used for many decades in the United States. Determinate sentencing was used prior to those decades, historically. More recently sentencing in the United States has been relying more upon determinate sentencing, when sentencing offenders in the corrections system.

Indeterminate sentencing was introduced in New York State in the early 1800's. The prisons were looking for a way to reward prisoners for good behavior. This was the introduction to the "good-time" laws. "In the United States, good-time laws emerged as early as 1817 in New York State, when prison administrators began asking their state legislatures for a way to reward well-behaved inmates." (Chambliss, 2011, p. 61).

Towards the mid 1800's indeterminate sentencing had taken off. Most of the States in the United States had implemented "good-time" laws, or indeterminate sentencing standards. These "good-time" laws were put in place to reward hard working prisoners. Those prisoners who worked hard, and maintained good behavior, would be given the chance to be released early from their prison sentence.

Indeterminate sentencing has an advantage for prisoners, as it allows the prisoners to work hard to rehabilitate themselves, to get released early from jail. Zebulan Brockway, a former warden of the Detroit prison system, felt that indeterminate sentencing was detrimental to the rehabilitation of prisoners. Brockway called this model the reformatory model. "Brockway felt strongly about the merits of what has been called the reformatory model. He advocated indeterminate sentencing as "quite indispensable to the ideal of a true prison system" and an essential part of his rehabilitative model." (Siegel, 2011, p. 19). Brockway felt that to create incentive for prisoners to want to reform, a step program should be made available. "The program was aimed at changing the prisoner's character, and the superintendent would then decide when the change in the convict's character justified release. All releases were conditional, and discharge depended on conduct while under supervision in the community over a period of six months." (Seigel, 2011, p. 19). Elmira, New York was the first prison to implement these policies.

Determinate sentencing, in theory, is the exact and polar opposite of indeterminate sentencing. Indeterminate sentencing may sentence a prisoner to 3-5 years, whereas, determinate sentencing the prisoner would serve a sentence of five years. Determinate sentencing is based on the model of mandatory sentencing. The prisoner is required to serve a minimum sentence, as required by statutory law.

Determinate sentencing is, however, not as it sounds. Determinate sentencing does, in some ways, mirror the model of indeterminate sentencing. Although the prisoner is sentenced to a mandatory minimum sentence, this does not incorporate "good time". Good time is an allotted time that corrections, and courts allow prisoners to deduct from their mandatory sentence. "Good time is a reduction in the time served, amounting to a certain number of days per month for each month served. If inmates obey the rules and stay out of trouble, they accumulate goodtime credit that accelerates their release" (Champion, 2008, p. 7).

The variance in the two models is minimal. With either structure of sentencing, the same, or a similar structure is put in place for prisoners to follow. Either school of thought seems to reinforce the concept that rewarding prisoners for good behavior is detrimental in the positive recovery, and rehabilitation of prisoners.

Although the determinate sentence seems to be the most preferred model of sentencing, historically, indeterminate sentencing has gained popularity over the years. This is due to the overcrowding of prison systems. The problem with indeterminate sentencing is that prisons seem to allow reduced sentences for lesser accomplishments. "However, 100 years later a rising crime rate created dissatisfaction with the indeterminate sentence and the treatment model. Conservatives disliked the apparent leniency of parole and early release, which seemed to link short sentences to good grades in school and satisfactory reports from work supervisors." (Seigel, 2011, p. 41). For this reason, determinate sentencing has the advantage over indeterminate sentencing. Determinate sentencing does allow for earlier release for "good-behavior", however, the main difference is that with determinate sentencing, the guidelines for early release are more defined, and are generally more regulated than those of indeterminate sentencing. This is the main reason why it seems as though determinate sentencing may have an advantage over indeterminate sentencing.

INMATE CUSTODY AND CONTROL

In the world of corrections, there are two fundamentals that must be exercised when dealing with inmates. These two fundamental tasks are the custody and control of prisoners in a correctional setting. Some of the methods used to maintain this custody and control are disciplinary procedures, physical layout of the facility, gang control, screening and classification, grievance procedures, use of force, administrative and leadership, humane institutions and staff training and education,

One way to maintain control of prisoners is through disciplinary actions and procedures. With disciplinary procedures, prisoners still carry minimal due process rights under the 14th Amendment of the Constitution. This is due to a 1974 ruling by the Supreme Court in Wolfe v. McDonnel. The Wolfe v. McDonnel Supreme Court ruling asserts that due process rights "were not equivalent to criminal prosecution and that during disciplinary hearings prisoners do not have the full due process rights of a defendant on trial. Nevertheless, the Court specified certain minimum requirements for disciplinary proceedings" (Siegel, 2014, p. 224).

The physical layout of the correctional facility also has bearing on the discipline and control of inmates as well. The physical structure of the facility has a direct influence on the behavior of the inmates, and how the guards are stationed in each prison. "Generally speaking, there are three basic types of jail design: linear intermittent surveillance, podular remote surveillance, and podular direct supervision." (Hutchinson/Keller, et. al, 2009, p. 11). Podular design seem to have the most positive impact on inmate behavior. In this design, the prison is open to one large common area, in which guards are stationed. With this design, guards are forced to have constant interaction with the population on a daily basis. This is not a common design in United States prisons, due to the old philosophy of containing prisoners.

Gang control, and screening and classification can generally be classified into one area. When prisoners are first brought into prisons, they are screened by prison officials to identify any gang affiliation. Control of the gang violence can possibly be minimized or prevented in the screening process. A proper gang screening should have a direct impact on the custody of the prisoner, as far as the unit the prisoner is housed in. If properly screened, it would be essential for prison officials to place members of rival gangs in separate housing units. This screening process alone, can effectively help reduce the amount of gang violence, and help keep order and control in each individual housing unit within the facility.

Grievance procedures are also helpful tools in the custody and control of prisoners. The process of grievance procedures helps prisoners feel as though they may have some control in their treatment. A grievance procedure is when a prison inmate is allowed to file a formal complaint against a guard, or member of the prison staff for mistreatment. "Grievances usually are submitted to someone in the institution and then go through a number of steps until they may end up in the director's office. If they cannot be resolved to the inmate's satisfaction on one level, they proceed to the next." (Seigel, 2013, p. 225). This process can help inmates feel vindicated in reporting their unjust treatment and may reduce the rate of attacks that may happen in retaliation to mistreatment by prison personnel.

The use of force is additionally a method used by correctional facilities in the United States. The use of force is highly regulated by law, and prison procedure. Many studies have been conducted by the Department of Justice, pertaining to the excessive use of force in prisons by prison personnel. These studies are the reason why use of force is now heavily regulated. This is held particularly true for adolescent males. "Federal investigators found that 308 of the 705 adolescent males in custody as of Oct. 30, 2012 — 43.7 percent — had been subjected to the use of force by staff at least once. The report notes that the number of injuries sustained by inmates has increased since then." (Greenblatt, 2014). The Department of Justice "report details a number of recommended changes, including revisions to use of force and solitary confinement policies, increasing supervision of staff and putting more cameras in areas housing adolescents." (Greenblatt, 2014).

Administration and leadership of a prison also plays a key factor in the custody and control of prisoners in a prison. Great leadership is one of the most important aspects to maintaining order and custody of prisoners. If the leadership is complacent with its approach in following procedure, this type of behavior may trickle down to the behavior of guards. In this case, even the structure of the prison facility may not prevent escapes, or violence within the prison walls. It is important for leadership, and the administrative team to remain professional and follow procedures that are implemented by the top tier of the chain of command. "Unquestionably, professionalism in corrections depends on the leadership of top administrators, including directors or commissioners of state or federal systems as well as wardens and superintendents of correctional institutions." (Seigel, 2013, p. 349).

Humane institutions, and staff training, and education are also two aspects of the custody, and control of prisoners that go hand in hand. The 8th Amendment allows for a prisoner to be free from inhumane treatment, as a basic right to all American Citizens. "Every inmate has the right to be free under the Eighth Amendment from inhumane treatment or anything that could be considered "cruel and unusual" punishment." (FindLaw, 2014). Proper training, and education of guards helps to facilitate humane institutions for prisoners and helps prevent prisoner abuse. This in turn also helps prevent hostility from prisoners, which aids in the control of the inmate population. In more modern times there is now a "realization that staff training is a necessary aspect of a humane prison." (Siegel, 2013, p. 202).

With the implementation of all the techniques stated, it makes the task of maintaining custody and control of prisoners a less daunting task. It is important to maintain custody and control of prisoners to effectively keep prisoners in prisons, and away from society, and to create a safe environment within prison walls for both prison personnel, and the inmates as well.

CLASSIFICATION PROCESS

The intake process is an elemental part to the safety, and security of prison systems in America today. A major part in the success in keeping prison systems safe, is the classification process used while doing intake on prisoners entering correctional facilities. When first entering a prison, prisoners "first experience usually occurs in a classification or reception center, where they are given a battery of psychological and intelligence tests and are evaluated on the basis of their background, offense history, personality, and treatment needs." (Seigel, 2014, p. 164).

The purpose for classification in prison systems

is to learn as much about the prisoner's true identity and behaviors. Classification investigates the behaviors, past criminal history, gang affiliations, medical conditions and mental and physical treatment needs. Identifying some of these factors and properly classifying prisoners "can reduce prison infractions and maintain a safer environment for both inmates and staff." (Hutchinson, 2015).

During classification a prisoner's medical history, and conditions are investigated by the intake unit. The intake unit may be looking to identify any mental disorders, contagious diseases, and any terminal illnesses a prisoner may passes when entering prison walls. This part of the intake process is pertinent to the proper housing of inmates for a few reasons. If an inmate has an infectious disease, it is possible for the inmate to not only infect other prisoners, but for the inmate to infect guards and prison personnel as well. Another aspect of the prisoner's medical history to take into consideration, is the prisoner's mental stability. For example, placing a schizophrenic inmate in general population would put that individual inmate, other inmates, and guards at risk of possible violent outbursts, or psychotic episodes. It is a crucial step in the classification of prisoners, to accurately research a prisoner's medical history.

Another part of the classification process involves classifying the prisoner's criminal history. Criminal history is a good indication of the pattern of behavior a criminal historically displays. A criminal with a history of violent felony arrests, will most likely be expected to act violently. An inmate with a history of only theft charges, would not be expected to execute violent behaviors, compared to an inmate with a violent criminal history.

Investigating a prisoner's background does not necessarily refer to criminal charges, but could also be the prisoners arrest record, and the prisoners prior, or current gang affiliations. A few sure signs to validate a prisoner's gang affiliation are; gang tattoos, prior gang related arrests, and an admission from the prisoner that the prisoner is, in fact, in a gang. "You can think of gang validation as a subset of security classification. Gang validation is the process that prison officials use to identify prisoners that they suspect of being members of gangs or "Security Threat Groups" (Skolnick, 2011). If a prisoner is validated as being in a gang, it is important for the safety of everyone to isolate rival gangs from being housed in the same units.

One more critical aspect of the classification process of prisoners, is to identify and isolate their treatment needs. This is an essential part of evaluating the prisoner's medical history as well. Identifying a treatment records is extremely essential, because a prisoner may need treatment for a terminal disease such as cancer, or the prisoner may require treatment for a drug, or alcohol addiction. For a person who requires treatment for an addiction, rapid detox could potentially kill an inmate, so certain special treatments are required.

In the State of Indiana, the Corrections system uses a scoresheet when evaluating a prisoner for classification. The scoresheet classification system was developed in conjunction with a collaboration between Indiana Department of Corrections, and the National Institute of Corrections. “The entire system was put in effect by February 1991 and has had a very positive effect on overall prison operations. Inmates are now being assessed and housed according to standardized criteria.” (Austin/Chan, et. al, 1993, p. 3). Since the implementation of a prison classification system, and a scoresheet to be used, Indiana has become more efficient in classifying offenders as they go through intake procedures while entering a prison. This has helped in the decrease of over classifying, and under classifying prisoners for effective placement in correctional facilities.

Overall, proper classification of prisoners when entering the prison system helps to reduce prisoner violence, the potential for escape, and the spread of communicable, or infectious disease within prison confines. The classification system not only helps keep prisoners safe from themselves, and other prisoners, it also helps keep prison personnel, and society safer as a whole.

SECURITY THREAT GROUPS

In most prisons in the United States, one of the biggest threats to security is prison gangs. “Prison gangs exist in 40 states and in the Federal Bureau of Prisons. In some states, especially California,

Illinois, and Texas, prison gangs are the dominant force in inmate life." (Seigel, 2013, p. 168). The five major gangs in prison consist of The Aryan Brotherhood, Black Guerilla Family, Folk Nation, Mexican Mafia, and MS13.

"The Aryan Brotherhood was founded by white supremacists Barry Mills and Tyler Bingham" (Associated Press, 2017) in 1964. The Aryan Brotherhood is a prison gang that consists of only white males. One of the main reason whites affiliate with the Aryan Brotherhood is to seek protection while incarcerated. The Aryan Brotherhood members will claim they join the gang to make their prison stay comfortable. Most of the activities of The Aryan Brotherhood, however, "are centered on drug trafficking, extortion, pressure rackets, and internal discipline." (Stohr/Walsh., 2015).

Geographically speaking, the Aryan Brotherhood "is the largest and deadliest prison gang in the United States, with 20,000 members inside prisons and on the streets. (Zinn, 2016). Most Federal prisons contain members of the Aryan Brotherhood. According to the Anti-Defamation League, the Aryan Brotherhood has its strongest roots in Texas. In the 1980's two white Supremacist groups merged to become the Aryan Brotherhood of Texas. "The Aryan Brotherhood of Texas (ABT) is one of the largest and most violent white supremacist prison gangs in the United States. ABT is responsible for committing dozens of murders and many other violent crimes." (Anti-Defamation League, 2013).

Black Guerilla family is another United States

prison gang that was founded in California's San Quentin State Prison. Black Guerilla family was founded in "the California Department of Corrections (CDC) in 1966 as the Black Family and Black Vanguard led by George Lester Jackson and W.L. Nolen. Jackson's group was first the Revolutionary Armed Movement (RAM) that aligned with the Black Panther Party, but he was locked up years before the Panthers started." (Morales, 2013). The members of the Black Guerilla Family are predominantly black prisoners. The Black Guerilla Family has also been known to spill out onto the streets as well. The Black Guerilla Family "is spreading from the prison system in Maryland to the street in a pretty rapid manner." (Ferranti, 2015).

On the streets, overall, the Black Guerilla Family is on the decline. "Originally to be a BGF in Cali one of the requirements was to have a life sentence. However, as some individuals were eventually released to the streets it was difficult to find the same level of individuals as in the prison system, so membership on the streets didn't blossom as it was a quality over quantity thing in Cali." (Ferranti, 2015). Due to the fact that the Black Guerilla Family is spreading into the streets of Baltimore, their geographical impact is most strongly represented in the Baltimore area.

In prison the ideology of the Black Guerilla Family is that of a political gang. On the streets of Baltimore, however, the gang concentrates mostly on the drug trade. The Black Guerilla Family in

Baltimore "are more into gangsterism than any type of political or black militancy so therefore it's a quantity over a quality thing. There are factions of BGF in Baltimore that are aligned more into the original political and militant ideology, just like a split occurred in Cali, there has been a split in Baltimore but can't elaborate further on that at this time." (Ferranti, 2015).

Folk Nation is another United States prison gang. The gang has its roots in Chicago and was founded by former Black Gangster Disciple Larry Hoover. According to the State of Florida, Folk Nation is not a gang. "The People Nation and Folk Nation are not gangs - they are alliances under which gangs are aligned." (Florida Department of Corrections, 2015). Some of the main gangs that the Folk Nation consist of are, Black Gangster Disciples, Black Disciples, Gangster Disciples, Imperial Gangsters, La Raza, Spanish Cobras, Latin Eagles, Latin Disciples and Satan Disciples. The Folk Nation consists mainly of Black and Hispanic.

The Folk Nation could be on an incline. Since the gangs' inception, it has spread across the United States, and as far South as Florida. The Gangster Disciples alone are "estimated to have over 50,000 members in the Chicago-city area, and 200,000 members in the country, and even 600,000 members world-wide." (Barnhart, 2009). Within the prisons, Folk Nation is involved in the drug trade, and organizing unrest. "Even in prison, Hoover gave orders to his gang members and directed their illegal drug trade. On July 22, 1978, an inmate riot at the Pontiac Correctional Center in Illinois resulted in the death of three corrections officers. This uprising was rumored to have been ordered by Hoover." (Barnhart, 2009). Their drug of choice being crack cocaine. According to online forums from the Folk Nation, their philosophy, or code is "all soldiers must share and respect a code of silence, loyalty to friends inside the nation." (Knox, 2004).

Additionally, the Mexican Mafia is also a violent prison gang within the United States prison system. "The Mexican Mafia prison gang was formed in 1957 at Deuel Vocational Institution (DVI) in Tracy, Calif." (Valdemar, 2007). The gang itself consists primarily of members who are of Mexican descent. Due to the increased violence of the gang, some members were transferred to San Quentin. This transfer of those prisoners helped increase the strength of the Mexican Mafia, by aiding in the growth of the gang into another facility.

According to the State of Florida's Department of Corrections, the Mexican Mafia, or "EME's philosophy centers on ethnic solidarity and control of drug trafficking (Florida Department of Corrections, 2015). The Florida Department of Corrections also states, "EME is the Federal Bureau of Prisons' most active gang, in terms of incident frequency rather than severity" (Florida Department of Corrections, 2015). Due to the frequency of incidents, the gang shows no signs of decreasing in strength or numbers. It seems as though the Mexican Mafia remains strongest in California.

In California, "the Mexican Mafia is believed to be the most powerful gang in Californian prisons, with up to 400 official members and around 990 associates who are involved with its criminal work and aspire to become official members." (Connolly, 2013).

Lastly, the MS13 is a violent force to be reckoned with, within the prison system in the United States. Ernesto Miranda founded the gang "MS-13 after immigrating to Los Angeles in the 1980s to escape the civil war in El Salvador." (Kim, 2006). The gang consists primarily of Salvadorian immigrants, and also Hondurans, Mexicans, Guatemalans, and member from other South American countries. The FBI classifies MS-13 as an International threat, and their numbers are growing. "MS-13 operates in at least 42 states and the District of Columbia and has about 6,000-10,000 members nationwide. Currently, the threat is highest in the western and northeastern parts of the country, which coincides with elevated Salvadoran immigrant populations in those areas." (Federal Bureau of Investigation, 2008).

The MS-13 gang is known for its violent philosophy. "MS-13 members engage in a wide range of criminal activity, including drug distribution, murder, rape, prostitution, robbery, home invasions, immigration offenses, kidnapping, carjackings/auto thefts, and vandalism. Most of these crimes, you'll notice, have one thing in common—they are exceedingly violent". (Federal Bureau of Investigation, 2015).

Gangs are perpetually one of the most violent

aspects if the prison system. MS-13, in particular, has a worldwide presence in prison system, and is known for their violent nature. In September of 2013, six MS-13 members were hung to death in a prison riot at a juvenile detention center. "Two of the dead were minors and four were adults who had been sentenced at a younger age. Police believe the murders were carefully calculated gang killings." (2014).

The threat of violence by prison gangs is a rampant problem within the United States prison systems. Knowing and understanding the mission, foundation, and criminal intentions of each gang is detrimental to gang violence prevention within the prison system, and on the street. The dangers of gang violence are ever present, however, knowing how to identify gangs, and gang members, is the best line of defense when it comes to preventing gang related violence within the prison community.

Chapter 3

Criminal Law

FEDERALISM

The Government of the United States is ruled by many laws and regulations. The founding fathers of this Country drafted some of the first laws of our land in the Constitution of the United States. To this day the U.S. Constitution governs most of the laws of the land. Case law, Codes, and Legislation is a determining factor in many judgments in Court proceedings, however, the Constitution is the back bone of many private citizen's rights. The Constitution also helps shape procedure on how individual States legislate their own laws.

Federalism is the basis behind The United States legal system. Each citizen is required to follow both the laws of the State and the Country. "Citizens are regulated by two separate governments, federal and state." (Hames/Akern, 2010, P. 19). The States have the power to legislate any laws within their own limits. Any laws that the States make, however, are not able to outweigh any laws that are legislated by the Federal government, including The U.S. Constitution.

When it comes to Jurisdiction, Federal Government has the Supreme power. This is a fact in many cases. Jurisdictions are broken down into two types of jurisdiction; Concurrent Jurisdiction, and Exclusive Jurisdiction. Exclusive Jurisdiction is defined just as the name implies, Exclusive. Exclusive Jurisdiction is "the sole power or authority to act in a certain situation." (Hames/Akern, 2010, p. 20).

One example of exclusive jurisdiction would be the printing of money. It is not possible for States to print their own money. The Federal Government has absolute Jurisdiction over the Printing of money. Concurrent Jurisdiction on the other hand, is Jurisdiction that either the state, or the Federal Government can claim jurisdiction over.

How are Jurisdiction issues dealt with between State and Federal Government? These issues of Jurisdiction are primarily handled through The U.S. Constitution. The U.S. Constitution has a Supremacy Clause which states in Article VI, "This Constitution, and the Laws of the United States which shall be made in Pursuance thereof. . . shall be the supreme Law of the Land; and the Judges in every State shall be bound thereby, any Thing in the Constitution or Laws of any State to the Contrary notwithstanding." So, the Supremacy clause is defined, again how it sounds. The United States Constitution reigns supreme over any state laws or Jurisdiction when in doubt.

All states within the United States, follow the United States Constitution. Each State also has a Constitution drafted as well. Each State is to also follow their own Constitution. The most important aspect is an American citizen's Civil Rights must never be violated. To insure this, each State is required to follow the law of The Bill of Rights, which was drafted by the Federal Government of the United States. Each State must abide by the Fourteenth Amendment of the Bill of Rights. Part of this Amendment declares, "nor shall any State deprive any person of life, liberty, or property, without due process of law." (Hames/Akern, 2010, p. 22). The Fourteenth Amendment ensures that all Citizens in The United States are treated equally in court proceedings, regardless of the U.S. State the individual is being tried in.

There are four types of laws in the United States Government Legal System. One of these types of laws is based off the principal of Stare Decisis. Stare Decisis are laws based off Precedents. Basically, this is how other cases were decided prior to the case that is presently being tried. This is an example of what is known as Case Law, or Common Law. One could speculate it is called Common Law, because it relates to cases that have an amount similar, or in common with another case.

The U.S Constitution, and the State Constitution are known as Constitutional law. These are a set of laws that were drafted by the founders of The United States, and the founders of each state. Statutory Law is law that is legislated into action. This requires votes to be passed when laws are presented to Congress to enact what are known as Statutes. Finally, the fourth type of law is known as

Administrative Laws. Administrative laws are drafted by Government agencies such as the IRS.

The United States Legal System is a complex system that is based off many different variables and procedures. This system is necessary to maintain a fair and just society. Our Legal system is modelled off thousands of years of Law and procedures in modern society, and over hundreds of years in this Country alone.

CRIMINAL LAW AND PROCEDURES

Criminal law in the United States is an issue that is necessary to create order in our society. In criminal law a defendant has basic rights that are put in place to protect their Civil Liberties. There are certain procedures that must be followed in order to make sure an accused person gets a fair trial, and a fair judgment when accused of a crime. For a person to be prosecuted for a crime, certain facts must be proven against them beyond a reasonable doubt.

One of the factors that is taken into consideration is Mens Rea. Mens Rea is referred to as "the mental element of a crime" (Hames/Atkins, 2010, p. 346). Sometimes Mens Rea is also referred to as the "guilty mind" (Hames/Atkins, 2010, p. 346). When a person commits a crime, this aspect refers to what the person's mental state was before, and as they were committing the crime itself. Professor Jessica Gauvin stated "the prosecution must prove Mens Rea. (Gauvin, 2014). Gauvin goes on to further note, four factors the prosecution can use to prove Mens Rea. If the crime was:

1. A PURPOSEFUL ACT.
2. A KNOWING ACT.
3. A RECKLESS ACT.
4. A NEGLIGENT ACT

These acts refer to a defendant's ability to form criminal intent while committing, or before committing, the accused crime. In very rare circumstances, the defendant is not able to form criminal intent. A defense attorney could argue that intoxication may be grounds to prove the defendant did not exercise mens rea. A counter to that defense could be that the defendant made the conscience decision to consume the drugs or alcohol that led to the intoxication. The only legitimate defense for a person accused of a crime, may be that the defendant was drugged without their knowledge, or the defendant was mentally incapable of exercising mens rea.

The prosecution must next prove actus reus. The act of committing the crime is known as actus reus. Actus reus can be more formally defined as "the second element of a crime: the guilty act or the physical act of the crime." (Hames/Atkins, 2010. p. 347). For actus reus to be proven against a defendant, the prosecution must prove that this was "a volitional physical act." (Gauvin, 2014). The second basic element of the crime must prove the person committed these acts voluntarily with their own physical actions.

For the defendant to be prosecuted, there must be concurrence between both mens rea and actus reus. What this means is, the prosecution must provide evidence to support the fact that the defendant, through their own actions and thoughts, whether through negligent acts or purposeful intentions, caused the crime to occur.

One case study where this can be examined is through the case of "Jacob Simmons". (Hames/Atkins, 2010, p. 344). In this case Ron Opal walked into an establishment that was being frequented by the defendant Jacob Simmons. In this case Jacob Simmons is to be charged with assault and aggravated battery. The prosecution has an easy burden to prove mens rea, and actus reus. By Jacob Simmons own admission, after he committed simple battery against Mr. Opal, Mr. Jacobs stated "Stay away from me, or you will be sorry." (Hames/Atkins, 2010, p. 344).

The defense could use the argument that Mr. Opal initially approached Mr. Jacobs and made an antagonizing comment, which in turn started the conflict. However, it could simply be argued by the prosecution that the comments made were no more than an expression of Mr. Opal's 2nd amendment rights, and not made in an assaulting manner. The Prosecution could also claim the actions of Mr. Opal did not justify Mr. Jacobs aggravated battery and assault of Mr. Opal. Mr. Jacobs attacked Mr. Opal with such veracity, using a weapon, this caused a wound on Mr. Opal that has left Mr. Opal in intensive care.

If Mr. Opal does not pull through, and ends up dying, Mr. Jacobs will also be facing possible manslaughter charges as well. Which mens rea, and actus reus are also easily proven. It was, in fact, Mr. Jacobs negligent actions that caused Mr. Opal to be in critical condition. This negligent and voluntary act was executed at the hand of Mr. Jacobs by his own admission, therefore leaving Mr. Jacobs accountable for the crimes.

Chapter 4

Case Studies

JON BENET RAMSEY

Jon Benet Ramsey was a six-year-old girl that was murdered December 26, 1996. Although police "found several other key pieces of evidence at the surrounding crime scene" (Crime Scene Museum LLC, 2014), the police have yet to find the killer in the case. The Ramsey investigation consisted of finding most of the four types of evidence; personal evidence, physical evidence, miscellaneous evidence, and corpus delicti evidence.

The first piece of evidence that was discovered was personal evidence. This was the initial report to the police that Jon Benet was missing. The second piece of evidence that was discovered was the corpus deliciti evidence. Finding the body was the first indication that the crime of murder was possibly committed. Finding her body triggered the start of the investigation into Jon Benet's murder. The investigation that followed entailed the collection of various pieces of physical evidence such as writing samples, boot prints, fingerprints, and pubic hair in a blanket. The Ramsey's never took a polygraph test and were never indicted for the crime. There was never any miscellaneous evidence to really be spoke of, or that would be admissible in the investigation.

One of the first pieces of personal evidence was when John Ramsey pointed out the physical evidence of the broken basement window to the responding officer. The physical evidence, in this case was a broken window in the basement of the Ramsey home. "Investigators don't know how long the window had been broken, but John Ramsey told investigators he had broken the window once when he locked himself out of the house." (Auge, 1999).

The broken window was considered out of the norm for a few reasons. First and foremost, John Ramsey was wealthy, and it was the middle of December. Secondly, it appeared the window was broken from the inside, yet there was scuff marks around the window as if someone had exited through the window. The fact that there are also scuffs around the window, and the window appears to be broken from the inside makes part of the crime scene look staged. The crime scene also appeared staged, due to the fact that spider webs were discovered outside the same window, and the webs were undisturbed.

The broken glass was pertinent to the initial investigation, because it basically set the tone for the rest of the investigation. The broken window was the first piece of evidence that made the crime scene appear as though it was staged. Another unusual piece of physical evidence was a three-page ransom note that was discovered at the scene. This was considered odd as well, because the note was written at the crime scene, and was also written on a pad that was at the crime scene. The handwriting analysis never cleared the mother of the crime and was considered inconclusive.

There were many pieces of physical evidence discovered at the crime scene that indicated the crime scene was staged. Many of the pieces of evidence gave indication that the Ramsey's themselves were possibly in on the murder. However, there were also "fingerprints, handprints, and a boot print that have still not been identified to the Ramsey's or anyone in their circle of over 400 people that have been investigated." (Crime Scene Museum LLC, 2014). The evidence at the scene appears to indicate that if the Ramsey's were involved with the crime, there may have also possibly been other perpetrators involved in the crime.

LEOPOLD-LOEB

The Leopold-Loeb case is a murder case from the early 1920's. The case involves two young teenage boys, Nathan Leopold and Richard Loeb, who were "obsessed with the idea of the perfect crime." (Osterburg/Ward, 2015). Leopold, and Loeb lured a younger teenage boy into their car, where the murdered the young man and later attempted to demand ransom.

In 1924 Leopold and Loeb had come up with a plan to commit a murder and get away with the crime. Leopold and Loeb had found a random victim, and stalked him, learned his patterns of travel, and decided to murder the boy. On the day they were supposed to murder the boy, he did not show. In a last-minute effort, Leopold and Loeb lured a different random 14-year-old boy into their car.

Subsequently Leopold and Loeb lured the 14-year-old victim into the vehicle, they killed the victim with a chisel. A chisel is a sharp instrument that would possibly have caused blunt force trauma, and lacerations. There is no mention, however, of blood being found in the vehicle. With a wound from a chisel, there should be an excessive amount of blood from the victim.

After Leopold and Loeb killed the victim, the stuffed the body in a culvert. When they were stuffing the body in the drain pipe, Nathan Leopold has apparently dropped a pair of his prescription glasses at the crime scene. "Police traced the glasses to a Chicago optometrist who had prescribed them for Nathan Leopold." (Osterburg/Ward, 2015).

The Police believed there was no motive for the crime. The only motive investigators believe there may have been was Leopold's obsession with committing "the perfect crime", and the "need to experience the ultimate thrill. (Osterburg/Ward, 2015). "Dillattantes and students of the fine art of murder think "the perfect crime" means circumventing the established hazards by concealing the motive, disguising the crime, and avoiding the consequences." (Osterburg/Ward, 2015). Prior to this murder, both suspects had only committed petty crimes in fraternity houses. The pair slowly graduated to more serious crimes and decided committing murder would be a big rush. This would have been the only possible motive to the crime, as they did not know the victim, and they were not doing it for ransom money. In spite of the ransom note, Leopold's "father's secretary was authorized to write checks up to $2,500 at his son's request." (Osterburg/Ward, 2015).

The heinous act that these two perpetrators committed would be ruled as a criminal homicide, or murder. "Murder is the unlawful killing of a human being with malice aforethought (premeditation)." (Osterburg/Ward 2014). Being that the suspects planned the whole killing out in advance, going as far as preparing alibis, this crime of murder was premeditated. A crime of passion, or manslaughter would simply be due to negligent acts, which the suspects were negligent, however, the malice and premeditation of the act makes this a straight murder charge. Suicide, which involves the killing of one's self is not comparable, nor is lawful homicide, as a lawful homicide would be a homicide that is used in a self-defense situation.

The Leopold-Loeb case was solved using the basic techniques of investigation. These techniques played a significant role in apprehending the suspects in this crime. The first technique that was used, playing to the advantage of the investigators, was to identify the body. Luckily, police found the body prior to the ransom note being sent. The police were also able to find the most solid clue, and were able to link that clue, Leopold's glasses, directly to the suspect by using people as a source of information. Using Leopold's medical records linked Leopold to ownership of the physical evidence.

One other key piece of evidence, although not as strong as the physical evidence found at the scene, was the information investigators received regarding the ransom note. Police investigators were able to pinpoint the font used on a typewriter, that one of the suspects used personally, to the font used on the ransom letter. Investigators were able to gather information about the typewriter, by conducting interviews with friends of the suspects, again using people as information.

THE LINDBERGH BABY

The Lindbergh Baby case was one of the most interesting cases from its time era. The case resulted in the death penalty of a perpetrator who was believed to be a lone assailant. The details of the Lindbergh Study include conflict of the three components of the Criminal Justice System, and incorporated the defendant's adjudication, sentencing, and his corrective sentence.

There seemed to be a conflict with the three components of the criminal justice system in the Lindbergh baby case. Conflicts in the case seemed to derive more from the police investigation of the crime. Most of the conflict stemmed from three different law enforcement agencies, who wanted to claim jurisdiction over the investigation. The agencies that battled over jurisdiction were, the New York Police Department, New Jersey State

Police, and the Federal Bureau of Investigation.

The battle over Jurisdiction appeared to originate from the fact that although the kidnapping took place in New Jersey, "A second ransom note was received by Colonel Lindbergh on March 6, 1932, (postmarked Brooklyn, New York, March 4)" (FBI.gov, 2014). The fact that the kidnapping took place in New Jersey, logically would allow New Jersey State Police to have Jurisdiction over the investigation. Complications came from the fact that all the remainder of the ransom notes, after the first note that was discovered in Lindbergh's nursery, were sent to and postmarked in New York. This gave New York Police Department jurisdiction, in reference to the crimes being perpetrated in New York State.

"On May 12, 1932, the body of the kidnapped baby was accidentally found, partly buried, and badly decomposed, about four and a half miles southeast of the Lindbergh home, 45 feet from the highway, near Mount Rose, New Jersey, in Mercer County." (FBI.gov, 2014). This discovery made the crime advance from being just a kidnapping, to a murder case in the State of New Jersey.

The Police involved in the case were very intent on doing their jobs. There was an intensive investigation, and the Police from all the Jurisdictions were eager to apprehend a suspect in the case. This eagerness was especially true, after the baby was discovered. "The child's body was face downward, covered with leaves and insects. It was little more than a skeleton, the outline of a form in a dark, murky heap of rotting vegetation. The left leg was missing from the knee down, as were the left hand and right arm." (Aiuto, 2015). David T. Wilentz, the Attorney General of New Jersey, stated after the child was discovered, "as I told you before, there are some cases in which a recommendation of mercy might do, but not this one, not this one. Either this man is the filthiest and vilest snake that ever crawled through the grass, or he is entitled to an acquittal."

The Lindbergh baby case was investigated for over two years. Multiple suspects were interviewed, however, there was a large amount of circumstantial evidence to put one man on trial. An information was drafted by the prosecution in New York, and in New Jersey for separate crimes. There was enough evidence to put one Bruno Richard Hauptman before a first appearance in New York State for extortion, and in New Jersey for Murder. Sometime during his court proceedings, the Governor of New York agreed to hand Hauptman over to New Jersey, where he would have his first appearance for murder charges.

Even with only circumstantial evidence, the case against Hauptman made it past the preliminary hearing and the arraignment and was adjudicated in a jury trial. The whole jury trial against Hauptman was deliberated in less than five weeks. At Hauptman's sentencing, he was sentenced to Death as the punishment for his crime.

Public opinion of the case, before the indictment was delivered, was that Hauptman, was guilty of the kidnapping and murder. Crowds of spectators gathered outside of the courthouse, awaiting the final decision of the jury, and the sentence from the courts. After the crowd was delivered the news that Hauptman was sentenced to death, they were ecstatic. "All the rest-the polling of jury, the sentencing—was lost in the throbbing fury of the pack until the courthouse door opened and the figured of four women and eight men, led by State troopers, trailed slowly down the steps. Once ore the pack cheered—not for the work well done that is required of all good citizens—but because the cry had been heard, its demand satisfied." (Hohenburg, 1935).

Hauptman's sentence was appealed by the Defense, and the Supreme Court upheld the lower Court's decision. From the time of Hauptman's sentencing, to the date of his execution, he was incarcerated in New Jersey. At this point, Hauptman was in the custody of the New Jersey Department of Corrections. Hauptman was in the custody of Corrections for a little more than one year. Hauptman's execution was eventually carried out on April 3rd, 1936.

The Lindbergh Baby Case garnished media attention all across America. The reason the Lindbergh Baby Case garnered so much attention, is mainly because Charles Lindbergh was a celebrity at the time of the kidnapping. Charles Lindbergh was even revered as an American Hero of sorts. "The Lindbergh case, the "Crime of the Century," is not so much about the kidnapped and murdered child as it is about America's hero, Charles Lindbergh, the first man to fly the Atlantic alone, in a small, fragile, one-engine airplane, a feat so venerated that the plane occupies a prominent position in the Air and Space Museum." (Aiuto, 2014). The Lindbergh Baby Case was such a well-known crime; it is listed on the official Federal Bureau of Investigations web site to this day.

The Criminal Justice system prevailed in the court of public opinion in the Lindbergh Baby case. The Police followed through, responded to the initial call, did an accurate investigation, and made the arrest of the suspected criminal. The arrest was followed by two first appearances in separate jurisdictions, New York, and then New Jersey. New Jersey Courts continued litigating the Lindbergh Baby Case through preliminary hearing, arraignment, all the way to adjudication and sentencing. Corrections in New Jersey continued with following the sentence that was ordered by the court, all the way up to the day the criminal was executed. If you believe Hauptman was guilty of the crime, then the Criminal Justice System worked flawlessly in solving The Lindbergh Baby Case.

PEGGY HETTRICK

Peggy Hettrick was a small petite redhead woman who was killed late one night on her way home to her apartment. There were many suspects in the case, however, the person that was accused and convicted, was later exonerated of the crime due to DNA evidence.

The Prosecutor of the case was able to get charges filed against the suspect Timothy Masters, eleven years later with the help of a criminal psychologist J. Reid Meloy. The Psychologist, "concluded that Masters' artwork implicated him in the crime." (Possley, 2012). "Armed with Meloy's report, Masters was charged with murder on August 10, 1998." (Possley, 2012).

The Prosecutor in the trial was amazing. He managed to get Masters convicted of the crime based on one cast of a footprint, and various pieces of circumstantial evidence. The Prosecutor in the case was "responsible for presenting the state's case against the defendant." (Schmalleger, 2015, p. 290). Prosecutors also "presented a raft of gruesome drawings and narratives of the torture, murder and sexual mutilation of women, which were seized from Masters during the long investigation." (Mitchell, 2012, p. 7). The Prosecutors did their job, and the Jury found the Defendant, Masters, guilty of the murder of Peggy Hettrick.

The Judge hearing the case had "the responsibility for safeguarding both the rights of the accused and the interests of the public in the administration of criminal justice" (Schmalleger, 2015, p. 287). The Judge did sentence Masters for the Murder Masters was found guilty of. The Judge must have followed proper court procedure in regard to maintaining fairness, because "Two years later the Colorado Court of Appeals upheld Masters' conviction and in 2002 the Colorado

Supreme Court likewise upheld his conviction narrowly." (Mitchell, 2012, p. 8).

The Defense counsel had their work cut out for them and followed through with their duties in the long run. Some of the "duties of the defense counsel include testing the strength of the prosecution's case, taking part in plea negotiations, and preparing an adequate defense to be used at trial." (Schmalleger, 2015, p. 293). The Defense took this a few steps further, and appealed the verdict many times, all the way until 2008. On January 22, 2008 Masters was released on bail, based off of new DNA evidence. The DNA evidence was the exculpatory evidence needed to exonerate Masters of the crime. "Two days later, Colorado Attorney General John Suthers took over the investigation of Hettrick's killing. The day after that, Larimer County District Attorney Larry Abrahamson filed a motion dismissing all charges against Masters." (Mitchell, 2012, p. 9).

NOTORIOUS B.I.G.

There are many suspects in the murder case of Christopher Wallace, aka the Notorious B.I.G. Christopher Wallace was gunned down in the streets of Los Angeles while sitting at a red light on the passenger side of a vehicle.

According to the FBI file, the person that is most likely to be charged with the murder is former LAPD Officer David Mack. If Suge Knight were to be arrested, he would most likely only be charged with conspiracy to commit murder. This is due to some evidence such as Knight's connection to the LAPD officer's working Security the night of the party. According to Kading, the lead LAPD Detective in the case, Knight's longtime girlfriend and business partner indicated he paid for the Wallace murder. "During one or more of [Swann's prison visits]. Knight instructed [Swann] to help him coordinate the murder of Christopher Wallace." (Vogel/Wilson, 2011).

The Prosecutor, theoretically, could charge Mack with Murder, and conspiracy to commit murder. Conspiracy to commit murder should be added to the charges, because conspiracy to commit will most likely be easier to convict on, if the Prosecutor cannot get the Murder charge to stick, or the Prosecution could possibly work a plea bargain with the defense. According to FBI reports, the first person to visit Mack in jail was "Amir", another suspect identified by witnesses in police lineups, and in sketches made at the scene, Since Mack is already incarcerated, Mack would be transported to his first appearance. At Mack's first appearance he would be advised of the charges being filed against him, and his right to retain council. Bail would not be an issue at the first appearance either, as Mack is already incarcerated for a violent offense.

In the next step of the process, the Prosecutor, could bring the case before a Grand Jury to decide if a crime has been committed. This must be done before the case could go onto arraignment and trial. During the Grand Jury trial, the Prosecutor would be allowed to call witnesses. The Prosecutor would call the jailhouse informant who identified "Amir" as the shooter, or one of the shooters. Prosecution would also call Forensic experts who can identify the rarity of the Gecko 9mm rounds found in Mack's home, that were also linked to the Biggie Smalls murder. Theoretically, it is virtually impossible to name all the witnesses that the Prosecutor could call, because the FBI report is highly redacted. The actual Prosecutor, however, would be afforded the names of the investigating officers who discovered the rounds, and the witnesses who can create the links between Suge Knight, "Amir", Officer Mack, and the other LAPD officers related to Knight, who were present at the VIBE After Party at the Museum.

The Prosecution's opening statement should demonstrate Mack's criminal history, his history of being a corrupt cop, his obsession with Tupac Shakur, and how witnesses have indicated the murder of B.I.G. was a Gang retaliation for Tupac's murder. Prosecution would also bring up the facts as to how the FBI report indicates Gecko 9mm ammo, which was only sold in L.A., and New Jersey, was used in the murder, and also found in Mack's home. It would also be important to stress the same style of vehicle that was used in the killing, according to witnesses, was registered to Mack at the time of the murder. Prosecution could also mention any ties Mack had to the suspected gangs involved in the "East coast/West coast Beef."

If possible, before bringing in Mack on the

charges, Prosecution should request for a forensic analysis be done on the 9mm rounds fired from the guns Mack had in his home and compared to the rounds found at the Wallace murder scene.

If the case made it to arraignment, the defense would have Mack plead innocent. Defense could call any, and all witnesses that would discredit Kading, as he was accused of corruption on a previous high-profile case. Defense would call on Mack to testify as well. Some of the witnesses listed in the FBI report were criminals facing charges, or jailhouse informants. Defense could also call every one of those witnesses, simply to discredit the Prosecution's case. Defense should also call any witnesses that could verify an alibi for Mack. Two more witnesses Defense would call were Suge Knight, and "Amir", if they actually had no connection to Mack. If they did in fact have a connection Defense should not call them. Defense would most likely hope the Prosecution did not call them as well.

The Defense attorney could, in theory, beat the murder charge, as most of the evidence is circumstantial, and direct evidence, based on witness testimony. If, however, the Prosecution was able to forensically link the bullets found at the scene, to the guns in Mack's possession, this would create strong forensic evidence. At that point, Defense would possibly start thinking about instructing Mack to take a plea bargain, if the forensic evidence was a match. Defense would ask for a plea before the trial makes it to closing arguments, and the jury had a chance to deliberate the verdict.

THE COATESVILLE FIRES

The Coatesville fire case, is a case in Pennsylvania where there was a string of arsons. In a one of the fires, a woman that was a Nazi camp survivor, lost her life. The case consisted of five preliminary arrests. Two of the main suspects were, a volunteer firefighter, and a 19-year-old student. The 19-year-old confessed to nine of the fires. In one, or both cases, probation could be an alternative to sending the suspects to jail.

To find out which suspects would be eligible for probation, the courts must take a few things into consideration. The first thing the court must do is a presentence investigation. A presentence investigation "examines the offender's background to provide the sentencing judge with facts needed to make an informed sentencing decision." (Schmalleger, 2014, p. 394). If either of the suspects that were arrested had prior criminal convictions for crimes, particularly similar crimes, probation may not be a good idea for a sentence from the courts.

The following step, if the suspects meet the requirements for the presentence investigation, is for the probation officers to do intake procedures. The intake procedures "involve a dispute-settlement process during which the probation officer works with the defendant and the victim to resolve the complaint before sentencing." (Schmalleger, 2014, p. 394).

After the probation officer meets with both the victims, and the accused, the probation officer would be required to do a diagnosis and a needs assessment. During the needs assessment process, the probation officer may decide that the accused needs to pay restitution to the victims of the crimes. In the case of the Coatesville fires, restitution should be required, as there was a great amount of property damage.

Another consideration the probation officer should consider for probation is a remote tracking bracelet for the offenders. Since the crimes were committed when no one was around, it would be relevant to be able to track the offenders' activity, if they are free in the community. Requiring a psychological test for the offender may also be warranted. A psychological test may also be a good indication to test if the client is able to partake in probation as a sentence.

Once all the proceeding steps have been accomplished, the judge may accept the recommended sentence of probation. At this point the probation officer would be required to conduct supervision of the clients. The probation officer is responsible for following up with the clients and making sure they follow the parameters set within their probation sentence. The probation officer may also conduct searches of the client's residence and conduct drug tests as well.

Specifically, for arson, another stipulation may be

that the offender not leave the state. When a judge sentences an offender, who committed arson to probation they "must comply with specific terms, such as regularly reporting to a probation officer, not leaving the state without permission" (Theorharis, 2015).

These are a few steps that should be followed by a probation officer when it comes to conditions that an offender must follow. Probation is often used as an alternative to prison sentences for offenders, including those convicted of arson. If the system is utilized properly, it can be an effective punishment for the offender, and save the taxpayers, and the courts both time and money.

Chapter 5

Psychology in Crime

CRIMINOLOGICAL PERSPECTIVES

Criminology is the study of the psychology behind crime, and criminal acts. There have been multiple studies to substantiate the psychology behind the criminal mind. These studies have come up with a multiple of theories regarding criminological studies. Three of these theories are biological/psychological, social, and choice theories.

Social theories can be broken down into a few different theories that researchers have discovered. Social disorganization theory is the first of these theories. Social disorganization theory speculates that criminals commit crimes because of the social and physical environments that they are a part of. This includes the social structure of the neighborhood in which they live. "In particular, a neighborhood that has fraying social structures is more likely to have high crime rates. Such a neighborhood may have poor schools, vacant and vandalized buildings, high unemployment, and a mix of commercial and residential property." (Briggs, 2009). With Social disorganization theory, the crimes that the criminal commits, may be based on the behavior of the neighborhood. Although this is a theory put out by researchers, this theory may seem nonsensical, in a way. This excuse seems to fall more under rational choice theory.

The next of the social theories is social learning theory. This theory seems to be a little more reasonable as to how the criminals learn to commit crime, versus, why the criminal may commit the crime. Social learning theory states that criminals learn how to commit the crimes, based off of the social circle that they associate with. Again, this theory seems to be a pre-requisite to rational choice theory.

The final social theory is social control theory. Social control theory propounds the ideas that most people in society would commit crimes if controls such as institutions, schools, places of employment, and churches were not in existence. Social control theory speculates, in part, that we all have a criminal mentality, or the propensity to commit crimes, but due to social construct we do not. This theory has a borderline Marxist, and communistic undertone. "Marx theorized that the work of producing consensus was done in the "superstructure" of society--which is composed of social institutions, political structures, and culture--and what it produced consensus for was the "base," the economic relations of production" (Crossman, 2011).

Rational choice theory, or choice theory, is another theory put into place by experts in criminology. Rational choice theory seems to be the actual underlying basis to a high amount of crime. This is based on reasonable interpretation, by law abiding citizens in society. Rational choice theory infers, with great reason, that criminals are self-serving. The choices that a criminal makes to commit a crime, is based off of the final outcome, or worst-case scenario. Criminals weigh the outcome of committing the crime, versus, the gain of committing the crime.

Lastly, trait, or psychological/biological theory is also another pliable theory as to why criminals commit crime. Psychological/biological theory can be broken down into two areas. First is the psychological part of the theory. The psychological aspect is based on the presumption that criminals may commit crime, because they have a psychological disorder such as schizophrenia. The next part of the theory is the biological side. Biological, and psychological are tied together, because many psychological disorders ore due to biological inheritance, or biological abnormality.

In the terms of psychological/biological theory, a criminal may have not consciously chosen to commit a crime. In cases where a criminal has committed a crime due to a psychological disorder, the punishment may be best served in the form of treatment to the criminal. Indeterminate sentencing for offenders suffering from aspects of the trait theory is widely accepted. "Some commentators, therefore, argue that those with the disorder are better managed in the criminal justice system, where, following the introduction of indeterminate sentences, engagement with psychological treatment is coercively linked to the achievement of parole." (McRae, 2013, p. 48). The sentencing for offenders who have committed crime due to psychological disorders, however, would fall under a different spectrum as the punishment, a "normal" offender should be sentenced to. Allowing a psychologically deficient criminal to be sentenced to a determinate sentence, unless it is a murder, or brutal rape, is simply just breeding an angrier psychologically abnormal criminal. It is pertinent to couple an indeterminate sentence for psychologically deficient criminals' sentence with some sort of psychiatric, or psychological treatment as well. The theory is to rehabilitate, more than punish the offender, with this type of scenario.

In direct contrast to trait theory, are offenders who consciously chose to commit their crimes based on personal gain. These offenders could be sentenced under a more punishment approach. Although, studies have shown that rehabilitation programs are effective when dealing with any inmates, the offenders that fall under choice theory should be sentenced accordingly. A determinate sentence for offenders who fall under the principles of choice theory could be more appropriate, particularly if the crimes are of a violent nature. The main difference in the rehabilitation, with these offenders, should fall more under the education type of rehabilitation. These types of rehabilitation programs, coupled with stiff sentences, should include educational programs, and work release programs. Parole could be possible for these offenders under the determinate sentence guidelines.

Any offender who falls under the social theory area of criminological theory, should also be treated the same as offenders who fall under choice theory. It is under my belief that even though these offenders may have been subjected to different environmental conflicts, these offenders still consciously chose to commit the crimes they committed. Thus, making the offenders reasoning for committing the crime a self-serving reason. The offender was consciously able to make the decision based on the reward, verse the risk of getting caught.

Regardless of the career one chooses in the field of Criminal Justice, criminology is an important field to know and understand. In some areas of Law Enforcement, a Criminology Degree, falls under the job requirements. "An undergraduate degree in sociology, social work, or criminology is required in most juvenile institutional settings. Many correctional systems also require the applicant to pass an intelligence aptitude test. To be promoted to social worker supervisor frequently requires a master's degree in social work, criminology, or sociology." (Seigel, 2013, p. 334).

Criminological perspectives, regardless of your opinion on each theory, helps shed a light on the mind of criminal offenders. Understanding the process behind a criminals' mind can help in the prevention, investigation, and the proper sentencing in crime. Therefore, any area within the Criminal Justice field could benefit from education, and training in the field of criminology.

The more law enforcement, and criminal justice employees know about the criminal mind, the better each individual will be in increasing their expertise within their field. Increasing the individuals' performance in their field not only helps that individual, but effectively helps influence, and create a stronger, more efficient team overall, and helps to make the criminal justice system more just and efficient.

Criminological Theory

Human before has a direct effect on the causation of crime. These effects all fall under criminological theories. There are many theories, but they break down to three main type e of causation. To evaluate the effect of human behavior involved within committing crime, the three main components of crime causation theories must be explored. These crime causation theories are biological, sociological, and psychological theories of crime causation.

Biological theories in crime causation, is the theory that humans commit crime due to genetic evolution, or the lack thereof. One such popular theory was put into place by Cesare Lombroso. Lombroso believed that human that committed crime were "throwbacks to earlier stages of evolution who were not sufficiently mentally advanced for successful life in the modern world." (Schmalleger, 2013, p. 78). This biological theory was known as atavism. Atavism was defined as; "A condition characterized by the existence of features thought to be common in earlier stages of human evolution." (Schmalleger, 2013, p. 78).

Particularly, Lombroso came to this conclusion, by studying a criminal by the name of Giuseppe Villella. "Lombroso conducted a post-mortem and discovered that his subject had an indentation at the back of his skull, which resembled that found in apes. Lombroso concluded from this evidence, as well as that from other criminals he had studied, that some were born with a propensity to offend and were also savage throwbacks to early man." (Mason, 2015). Therefore, Lombroso believed that the propensity to commit crime, was an inherited trait, passed down through the generations. This biological theory suggests; crime was committed due to lack of evolution of the criminal's human body.

Sociological theory of crime causation is also another theory that is popular amongst researchers, as to why individuals commit crime. Sociological theory is formulated around the assumption that crime is committed due to an individual's relationship to a particular subculture. Sociological theory can also relate the causation of crime to the environment in which the individual was raised in. For example, an individual who grew up around gangs, may be more likely to commit crimes due to peer pressure. Also, individuals who grew up in poverty in a neighborhood where the buildings are in distress, may also be more like to commit crime.

Part of sociological theory of crime causation, encompasses what are also known as environmental theories. “The main idea developed from this theory is the "broken windows" thesis, which states that run-down and deteriorated buildings produce a delinquent attitude among residents.” (Osterburg, 2012, p. 340). There are police agencies that have implemented community policing programs based around the broken window theory. “Some police departments have, in fact, invoked “broken windows” as the rationale for zero-tolerance order-maintenance policing and have claimed to reduce crime by those police practices.” (Delattre, 2011, p. 361). There is yet to be any solid evidence, or data to confirm that fixing the building within a community, based on broken windows theory, has an actual reduction in crime for that area of policing.

For teen, sociological theory of crime causation can also manifest in the form of what is known as peer pressure. There were rallies held in youth day, 2016 to address these issues. One 12th grade, teen author gave this example; “The majority of the young people who start smoking/drugs and get arrested is because of peer pressure.” (Maswanganyi, 2016, para. 4). These pressures may also manifest in gang culture for adults, as well. Psychological theories of crime causation are theories that are based on the mental approach of crime causation. A psychological theory differs from a sociological theory, in the fact that these theories focus more on the individual. A psychological theory focuses more on internal factors, whereas, the sociological theories focus more on external factors. Psychological theories are more of a "perspective on criminological thought that views offensive and deviant behavior as the product of dysfunctional personality." (Schmalleger, 2013, p. 84.)

In early psychological theory research, there were two main focuses of psychological theory; behavioral conditioning, and personality. Behavioral conditioning operates on the theory that "the frequency of any behavior can be increased or decreased through reward, punishment, and association with other stimuli." (Schmalleger, 2013, p. 84). Personality focuses more on abnormal psychology, such as diseases of the mind. Personality also focuses on the "relatively stable characteristic patterns of thoughts, feelings, and behaviors that make a person unique, and that influence that person's behavior." (Schmalleger, 2013, p 84).

With psychological theories, the individual may not have the same cognitive functioning as the psychologically typical person within society. There are cases where people with mental disorders are referred to inpatient treatment, versus prison time. These individuals may not understand the difference between right and wrong and may not understand the cause and effect of their actions. In rare cases, some of these individuals are ruled incompetent to stand trial. There was a ruling involving a man in Wisconsin, where he was deemed unfit to stand trial. "The ruling followed the opinion of Deborah L. Collins, director of the Wisconsin Forensic Unit, who determined that Rozewicz did not have the ability to understand the charges and aid in his defense." (Luthern, 2016, para. 4). Therefore, psychological theories focus on the psyche of the individual committing the crime, not to include any external factors, for the most part.

All three theories may have a different effect on human behavior. In the examples posted above, each theory was taken into consideration. For biological theories, researches conducted posthumous autopsies on criminals. With sociological theory, teens involved within the pressure of outside social influence have weighed in on the topics. Pertaining to psychological theory, the courts have taken criminals psychological condition, and mental illness into account on many cases. Each theory may have a different effect on an individual. Some people who are raised in a negative social structure, are still able to maintain a positive approach to life, and not commit crime. For others, within, the same environment, the pressure may be too much, and their internal weakness allows for them to commit crime due to external pressure. In conclusion, each theory may have relevance to behavior within society, however, each theory may affect each human differently.

Chapter 6

Policing Styles

STYLES OF POLICING

In law enforcement, there are two main style of policing, when it comes to dealing with and responding to crime. Both community-oriented policing, and problem-oriented policing have been in effect for many years. It should be noted that each style of policing has its own cons and drawbacks.

Community oriented policing was started before the implementation of problem-oriented policing in many, if not all jurisdictions of law enforcement. There are many principles to implement when using this technique of policing. "However, since the advent of community policing, there is actually no universally accepted definition" (Yero/Othman et. al, 2011, p. 51). The United States Department of justice has classified community-oriented policing using their own definition. "Community policing is a philosophy that promotes organizational strategies that support the systematic use of partnerships and problem-solving techniques to proactively address the immediate conditions that give rise to public safety issues such as crime, social disorder, and fear of crime." (Department of Justice, 2012).

There are quite a few advantages to police

departments when implementing community-oriented policing. One of the main benefits of community-oriented policing is community relations between the officers, and the citizens. The police in these areas may be received as being friendlier, or more a part of the community, versus, being considered the enemy. Police may implement foot patrols, to get to know members of the community personally, and implement resource officers within the schools, to build relationships with the citizens of the community. The police may also implement organization such as community patrols, where citizens report directly to police on issues, or crimes they observe within the community. The biggest advantage to the community within community-oriented policing is, the members of the community may feel more empowered.

In studies that have been conducted regarding community-oriented policing there are mixed results. In a federal study, community-oriented policing proved to be effective across the board. "Zhao, Scheider, and Thurman (2002) found that COPS funding reduced property and violent crime in large U.S. cities. Likewise, Evans and Owens (2007) found that the police supported through COPS funding generated statistically significant reductions in auto thefts, burglaries, robberies, and aggravated assaults." (OJJDP, 2010, p. 4). In these studies, that were conducted, community-oriented policing had a substantial impact on lowering crime within communities.

As with anything, there may also be some drawbacks to the implementation of community-oriented policing as well. Although some studies have showed a significant reduction in crime, other studies have garnered contrasting results. In more recent studies, scholars who conducted a study in community-oriented policing produced a different, less significant impact regarding the results of community-oriented policing. "Although our analysis suggests that COP is associated with between 5% and 10% greater odds of a decrease in crime, it is plausible under the confidence intervals that COP has no effect on crime. We also find no evidence that community policing decreases citizens' fear of crime, despite positive outcomes for other citizen perceptions. Finally, our results do not suggest that the presence or absence of a problem-solving approach as part of COP strategies affect the impact on crime." (U.S. Dept. of Justice, 2015).

Problem oriented policing is a different approach to the problem of crime within a community. The United States Department of justice also has its own interpretation of the definition of what problem-oriented policing is. "Problem-Oriented Policing (POP) emphasizes the use of analysis and assessment to address crime and disorder problems" (U.S. Dept. of Justice, 2015). With problem-oriented policing, police officers are not just acting on call and respond tactics when dealing with crimes. "New officers are being trained (and older ones re-trained) to recognize the signs of problems rather than individual incidents." (Vincent, 2011).

Problem oriented policing has proven to be extremely effective in known high crime areas. There are many advantages in problem-oriented policing, one of those advantages is the lowering of crime within high crime areas. Statistics in past studies show drastic crime reduction in known crime areas with the implementation of problem oriented policing styles. "In one case, burglaries in the New Briarfield Apartment complex were reduced by 35 percent. In another example of problem solving, robberies in the central business district were reduced by 40 percent" (Eck/Spelman, 1987).

Even with the positives indicated in studies about problem-oriented policing, there are also studies that indicate substantially different results. "A recent Campbell Collaboration meta-analysis on the effectiveness of POP (Gill, et al. 2014) concluded that, while effect sizes are modest, POP is effective in reducing crime and disorder. Gill and colleagues identified 10 studies that met the inclusion criteria for the meta-analysis, a number they found surprisingly small given the widespread support for POP." (Gill, et. al, 2014). Although, it should be noted, these studies suggest a negative connotation with the results of these researchers. It should be taken into consideration that the results of their studies still indicate a positive overall reduction in crime under the implementation problem-oriented policing.

Each of the two styles of policing, community-oriented policing, and problem-oriented policing, both have positives and negatives within their implementation according to researchers. With the comprehensive analysis of both styles of policing, even within the research that experts viewed as negative results, there was still a reduction of crime. Regardless of what style a department chooses to implement, choosing to improve the training within the department, to reduce crime overall, is a positive approach to policing. This positive effect has a long-lasting influence on the morale, and well-being of not only the community served, but the well-being of the officers implementing these techniques on a routine basis. It seems that in either instance, change is a good change when it comes to implementing these styles of policing.

ROLES IN POLICING

When it comes to policing, there are many strategies that can be implemented. "There are five core operational strategies—preventive patrol, routine incident response, emergency response, criminal investigation, and problem solving—and one ancillary operational strategy—support services." (Schmalleger, 2015, p. 165). What are these strategies, and how are they effective?

Routine incident response

Objectives of:

- *Restore order*
- *Document information*

- *Provide immediate services to the parties involved*

Routine incident response is the second most frequent form of policing. “Most reactive police business is handled using routine incident responses which entail the methodical collection of information about a situation, and classification of the situation.” (Scott, 2000). These are calls that a police officer may respond to such as domestic disputes, or petty theft.

Emergency Response

Reasons for Response:

- *Crimes in Progress*
- *Traffic accidents w/ serious injury*
- *Natural disasters*
- *Terrorism incidents*
- *Officer request for assistance*
- *Incidents where a human life may be in danger*

Emergency response is a more serious part of policing, but with a less frequent occurrence than a routine incident response. “Police use emergency responses far less frequently than routine incident responses, yet they are probably the most critical to the police agency's success, because human life is most directly at stake.” (Scott, 2000)

Criminal investigation

The process of:

- *Discovering evidence*
- *Collecting evidence*
- *Preparing evidence*
- *Identifying evidence*
- *Presenting evidence*

Criminal investigation is the part of Policing that entails gathering evidence to solve a crime. This work is generally done by Detectives, but the investigation can be started with the Patrol officer. "Criminal investigations, while constituting a smaller proportion of police work than most people imagine, dominates the public's (and the police's own) perception of police work. "(Scott, 2000)

Problem solving

Better known by the acronym 'SARA'

- *Scanning*
- *Analysis*
- *Response*
- *Assessment*

Problem solving is the theory of stopping crime before it happens, using community outreach. Police identify problems, and refer residents, or potential criminals to community-based programs. "The general objective of problem-solving is to reduce harm caused by patterns of chronic offensive behavior." (Scott, 2000)

Preventive Patrol Analysis

Preventive patrol is the most common form of Police work. A majority of the day for an Officer is spent doing routine patrols. The two purposes behind a Preventative patrol are, "the presence of a uniformed police officer is intended to deter citizens from committing offences, and to enhance their sense of security." (Scott, 2000).

Preventive patrols are the basis, or foundation of all Police work. "Police patrol operations remain principally structured around preventive patrol, emergency response and the handling of routine incidents." (Scott, 2000). With effective Preventive patrols, it is also easier for Police officers to respond to routine patrols, and emergency response calls. If the officers are strategically located within their Preventive patrols, response time is minimalized when the officers respond.

Chapter 7

Juvenile Crime

JUVENILE DELINQUENCY: THE CAUSE?

Statistics and data are important factors to determine the causation of Juvenile Delinquency, and why Juveniles are more likely to commit crime. Children who come from broken, or single parent homes are more likely to commit crimes, compared to children from dual parent homes, invalidating the assumption that race plays a factor.

To help prevent or curb juvenile delinquency, the cause behind why these crimes are being committed is the key to prevention. One of the main problems lies in the upbringing of the children, and the fact that the juveniles come from single family homes. “Douglas Smith and G. Roger Jarjoura, in a major 1988 study of 11,000 individuals, found that "the percentage of single-parent households with children between the ages of 12 and 20 is significantly associated with rates of violent crime and burglary." (Fagan, 1995).

Some people might think that race plays a role in juvenile crime statistics. The fact is, socioeconomic status has more of a bearing on a child’s success. A successful child is less likely to commit crime. This appears to tie in to single parent families as well. A single parent family has less time than a dual parent family to spend with the children overall. The socioeconomic factor also holds true in families of higher income. Higher income families are able to spend more time with their children as well. “Affluent parents talk to their kids three more hours a week on average than poor parents, which is critical during a child's formative early years.” (O’Brien, 2014). This is putting children from lower class backgrounds at a disadvantage overall in life, not only just when it comes to juveniles committing crime.

Juveniles who come from broken homes statistically are more likely to commit crimes for other reasons as well. One of these reasons is, “the professional literature is overwhelming: teenage criminal behavior has its roots in habitual deprivation of parental love and affection going back to early infancy.” (Fagan, 1995). This correlates with the economic factors that are mentioned above as well. It would appear juvenile crime is a product of a child’s inability to gain love and attention in a healthy manner. Therefore, the child must act out, sometimes in a criminal manner to garner attention from whoever may be willing to offer it, even if these people are fellow peers who are also Juvenile Delinquents.

Children from lower economic status and broken single parent homes are more likely to be juvenile delinquents than children who come from affluent families. One method of prevention for Juvenile Delinquency may simply just be education of parents, and education of children from the infancy stage. Education of the whole family as a unit, may help deter crime overall as a society, starting with child offenders.

SOCIAL LEARNING THEORY AND JUVENILE CRIME

Social Learning Theory was introduced as a causation of crime patterns by Albert Bandura. Bandura believed that "behavior is learned from the environment through the process of observational learning." (McLeod, 2011). Social Learning Theory would contend that juveniles commit crimes by learning the behaviors from what they witness, and commit crimes because of the economic and environmental status the children are raised in.

In the Social learning theory Bandura theorizes that a child's behavior is a product of what the child sees. For example, a child who grows up in poverty may witness and see more crime, compared to a child who is raised in a more upper-class neighborhood. This may make the child feel that committing crime is more acceptable, because it is the social norm of the people the child is in constant contact with. The children use these people as models for their behavior. "These models provide examples of behavior to observe and imitate, e.g. masculine and feminine, pro and anti-social etc." (McLeod, 2011).

The Nurture theory is similar to The Social Learning theory. Nurture Theory postulates "if educational environments could be improved, the result might be both an elevation in IQ scores and a decrease in delinquency" (Siegel/Welsh, 2015, p. 89). "People can learn by observing the behavior of others, as well as from the consequences of those behaviors." (Kretchmar, 2008). Both ideas are very different from Nature Theory, which believes "that intelligence is inherited and is a function of genetic makeup." (Siegel/Welsh, 2015, p. 89). Nature Theory makes the presumption that juvenile offenders commit crimes because they are mentally deficient. "In 1926, William Healy and Augusta Bronner tested a group of delinquents in Chicago and Boston and found that 37 percent were subnormal in intelligence" (Siegel/Welsh, 2015, p. 89). Even if Nature theory was conclusive, the study contradicts the theory as well. The study would make only one in three juvenile offenders be of lower intelligence, according to the data the researchers compiled.

It would seem more logical to believe that Juvenile crime is a component of a child's environment. To assume that most juvenile offenders have lower I.Q. because of genetics seems to be a little baseless, as there are no Scientific DNA studies to back the Nature Theory as well. It would be safer to hypothesize that children, including juvenile offenders are a product of their environment, and do commit criminal behaviors because of the economic or environmental status in which they are raised in and around.

JUVENILES AND GANGS

Gang activity in The United States is a serious problem, even when it comes to Juvenile offenders. With the implementation of community-based outreach programs, counseling, and problem solving policing styles, the United States can help effectively minimize the number of violent juvenile delinquents in America today.

One of the issues with children in gangs today is based off of the antisocial behaviors that children demonstrate. Antisocial juveniles, or juveniles who do not have many friends, are more susceptible to becoming members of gangs. "In some instances, the peer group provides the social and emotional basis for antisocial activity. When this happens, the clique is transformed into a gang." (Seigel/Welsh, 2015, p. 215).

Some antisocial behaviors that may be a warning sign to parents and teachers are, sometimes small groups of an ethnic minority in an area are prone to become gang members. On occasion, "a gang may form when members of an ethnic minority join together for self-preservation." (Seigel/Welsh, 2015, p. 219). When there is an ethnic minority group, juveniles can clique together and create a turf for the 'gang' to protect, creating a safety net for this sub group.

According to Dr. Tom O'Connor, the Program Manager of Criminal Justice and Homeland Security at Austin Peay State University, the three most common antisocial disorders for criminal delinquents are: Antisocial Personality Disorder, Sociopaths, and Psychopaths. "Antisocials come is all shapes and sizes, and psychologists consider the juvenile version of it to be a juvenile conduct disorder. The main characteristic of it is a complete and utter disregard for the rights of others and the rules of society." (O'Connor, 2015). These types of mental disorders create the perfect recipe for a juvenile to be directed into gang style living.

A high percentage of juvenile delinquents have Antisocial Personality Disorder. Early identification and psychological treatment may be one strategy to combat delinquency. Antisocial Personality Disorder is very common in criminals, "the field of criminology tends to treat Antisocial Personality Disorder as so synonymous, in fact, with criminal behavior that practically all convicted criminals (65-75%) have it" (O'Connor, 2015).

Another hypothesis for the relationship of juveniles to gang involvement is "the association between gang membership and delinquency is unquestioned, there are three different explanations for the relationship:

- ***Selection hypothesis***. Kids with a history of crime and violence join gangs and maintain their persistent delinquency once they become members.
- ***Facilitation hypothesis***. Gang membership facilitates deviant behavior because it provides the structure and group support for antisocial activities.
- ***Enhancement hypothesis***. Selection and facilitation work interactively, increasing the likelihood of enhanced criminality" (Siegel, 2015, p. 229)

There are many proactive solutions to help prevent gang activity. Tracking gang crime statistics is a technique that can be implemented, in order to help Police, isolate the areas that need the most attention. Once police isolate these areas, they can proactively refer gang members to community outreach programs implementing a more problem-solving style of policing or make the appropriate arrests. Finally, "Professional respect and appropriate collaboration between Police and outreach workers and other team members are essential." (U.S. Dept. of Justice, 2010).

Social workers, Teachers, and Police Officers can help proactively reduce juvenile delinquency, and gang activity by looking out for all of these signs. Referring Juveniles to the right community resources, and programs when signs of APD, Sociopath, and Psychopathy behaviors are present, Community Leaders, Teachers, Parents, and Police Officers, can proactively help reduce gang violence for our youth.

EVOLUTION OF THE JUVENILE JUSTICE SYSTEM

The juvenile justice system is a system of criminal litigation specifically designed for juveniles. The juvenile justice system has undergone many changes since its early inception in the United States. These changes have helped to incorporate parental involvement, give the juveniles more due process rights, and create a more just legal system for juvenile offenders.

One of the most notable milestones in the change of the juvenile system was in the 1960's. It was at this point that the juvenile justice system moved from parens patriea philosophy, to more of a philosophy that allows more due process rights for offenders. "The key case was that of Gerald Gault; it articulated the basic requirements of due process that must be satisfied in juvenile court proceedings." (Seigel, 2014, p. 369). This heled to secure more Constitutional rights for juveniles. Under the prior parens patriea model, juveniles were not even afforded the right to counsel in defense for their crimes. Not only is this case a significant milestone in the evolution in the juvenile justice system, but it is also a historical ruling. This has helped shape the opportunity for defense counsel, rights against self-incrimination, and the right to confront the accuser as well.

The next historical milestone, in the form of a ruling by the Federal Supreme court is the decision of Roper v. Simons. "U.S. Supreme Courts holds the Eighth Amendment's ban against cruel and unusual punishment prohibits teens from being sentenced to death for crimes they committed before they reached age 18 in Roper v. Simons." (Backes, 2012). Roper v. Simons is a specific example of a ruling that helps to enforce a juvenile offender's Constitutional rights. Prior to this ruling by the U.S. Supreme court, a juvenile was able to be sentenced to death.

Another specific, and significant example of a historical landmark ruling happened more recently. In 2012 Federal courts made a ruling that was based off of Roper v. Simons. The ruling in 2010 elevated the rights of juvenile offenders in relation to sentencing. In Graham v. Florida, "Court abolishes the sentence of life without the possibility of parole for youth. Convicted of non-homicide crimes in Graham v. Florida, building on the building on the reasoning it applied in Roper (2005)" (Backes, 2012).

The Juvenile justice system today is greatly increasing in its stability and is more effective than it was more than 50 years ago before the Gault ruling. Whenever a U.S. citizen has to sacrifice their Constitutional rights in court, the court can easily be deemed ineffective. Since these historical rulings have taken place and created an evolutionary pattern of change in the juvenile justice system, juveniles have now been afforded the opportunity to exercise their Constitutional rights more frequently in court proceedings. Regardless if you are an adult, or a juvenile, the liberties afforded in the Constitution are the principles that the United States justice system is supposed to rely on for a fair day in court.

Chapter 8

Cyber Awareness

EMERGING TECHNOLOGY

Law enforcement, throughout history, has made it a priority to keep pace with advancing technologies. In modern times, this entails that law enforcement keeps pace with computer related technologies, in the field of criminal investigation. There are specific advantages, and disadvantages of law enforcement keeping up to date on computer and software related technologies. These tools in technology have also been used by criminals in different criminal enterprise, and likewise used by law enforcement in the prosecution of criminal cases.

The emergence of computer, and software technology has become an asset to the law enforcement community over the last decade. One major advantage of the use of computers, by law enforcement agencies, is the ability to help in predicting crime patterns. One such piece of software is known as CrimeStat. According to Levine (2002); "CrimeStat, a Windows-based spatial statistics-analysis software program for analyzing crime-incident locations." This software allows for the automatic analyzation of data, based on specific areas within a department's jurisdiction.

The use of this computer-based software is not only advantageous because it predicts higher crime areas, the software is also a major asset, because it saves man hours, in the calculations of the statistics.

There are many other computer-based software programs on the market, that are also utilized by law enforcement, as well. One of the other software technologies that has proved useful, in the investigation of crimes, is video analytic software. Video analytic software adds to prior technology of the video camera, or the eye in the sky. "Officers can do this manually, but as images proliferate, law enforcement has been increasingly turning to video analytic software that can sort through thousands of pictures to look for a specific image. This involves use of sophisticated software that recognizes faces or specific shapes and colors." (Schmalleger, 2014, p. 12). Again, utilizing this software in automatic mode, versus manual mode, is a resource saving tool, which saves departments money and time.

With all the many advantages to computer-based software technology in law enforcement, there are also disadvantages in the use of these software programs. Onc major disadvantage may be in the 9-1-1 call center of the police station. With the use of computer-based software, mostly all 9-1-1 calls are routed through a computer, when the operator answers the call. For the most part, there are many advantages to this type of software, but there may also be two major disadvantages to this software-based call system as well.

In the presence of a power outage, generators

may need to be obtained, to keep the 9-1-1 call center operational. If, however, the 9-1-1 call center is based off internet-based software, even with a generator, the technology become virtually inoperable. This can be a catastrophic failure in life and death situations. This applies to both the caller, and the officers who are out on patrol.

Police departments in St. Louis, Missouri have already adopted this patrol car tracking technology, and it is tied directly to the 9-1-1 system. "For about 10 years, St. Louis County police supervisors and dispatchers have been able to see patrol cars' locations, using laptops in their vehicles." (Byers, 2012, para. 20). It is for safety issues, that departments may already thinking of ways to upgrade these technologies. According to Byers (2012), St. Louis County is in the process of updating their patrol cars with Global Positioning Satellite (GPS) technology. Up until this point, the software system has relied upon laptop location, transmitted through the internet. This has proven to be a disadvantage, compared to current technology, and it is for that very reason the department is upgrading to GPS.

Another disadvantage to computer-based software technology may be the sheer cost incurred by the purchase, and upgrade of computers, and computer software equipment. There are many forensic computers, and software programs that cost thousands of dollars. Although, the department may be saving man hours in some investigative work, these hours need to be reallocated for proper training of the new computer technologies, and software, and updating the technology to keep it current, to stay up to speed with computer based technological crimes.

Computer based software can also be created, in order to assist criminal enterprise, in the commission of a crime. "In one phase of an insurance fraud in Los Angeles in 1973, a computer was used to model the company and determine the effects of the sale of large numbers of insurance policies. The modeling resulted in the creation of 64,000 fake insurance policies in computer-readable form that were then introduced into the real system and subsequently resold as valid policies to reinsuring companies." (Lukens, 1999, p. 25). Therefore, not only can computers, and computer software be used to assist law enforcement, the criminal element also possesses the ability to utilize this technology in a nefarious manner.

Just as criminals are able to utilize these new technologies in the commission of a crime, law enforcement has been able to use technology in the prosecution of criminal cases. For example, in 2016, Florida police were able to get a murder conviction of a man, using a picture he posted on, the popular social networking site, Facebook. "A Florida man convicted of second-degree murder after killing his wife and posting a photo of her blood-spattered body on Facebook was sentenced to life in prison on Friday." (Izadi, 2016, para. 1). According to a Reuters report, the man "posted an image of her bloodied body on Facebook shortly after the shooting." (Izadi, 2016, para. 13). Utilizing this simple form of technology, police were able to get the man sentenced to 20 years total, without parole.

INTERNET SCAMS

The internet is filled with many opportunists. These opportunists sometimes take advantage of people using internet scams. One common scam is called phishing. In 2006, the Federal Trade Commission published an article to help consumers, and first responders understand what they can do to protect against phishing scams. Auction sites like Ebay, also have protection for consumers from internet scams as well.

Phishing is when "thieves use false e-mail return addresses, stolen Web page graphics, stylistic imitation, misleading or disguised hyperlinks, social engineering, and other artifices to trick users into revealing personally identifiable information." (Muraski, 2013, p. 359). The Federal Trade Commission gives examples of emails that a consumer may receiving, when the consumer is being set up for a phishing scam. "We suspect an unauthorized transaction on your account. To ensure that your account is not compromised, please click the link below and confirm your identity." (FTC, 2006). The previous statement is an example of an email a consumer may receive.

The Federal Trade Commission has a few suggestions for a consumer, to help safeguard themselves against these types of email phishing scams. A few things the Federal Trade Commission suggests a consumer can do is, do not reply to the email, and delete the emails, or text messages. The best protective measure, however, is not to even open the email, if the email looks suspicious. The scammers will sometimes include a telephone number for consumer to call back in the phishing email. Even if the area code is local, consumers should not call the phone number that is listed within the email. “Some scammers ask you to call a phone number to update your account or access a "refund." But a local area code doesn’t guarantee that the caller is local.” (FTC, 2006).

Some other steps the Federal Trade Commission recommends are to use security software on your computer, do not email personal information, only provide personal information through an organizations website, review credit card, and bank transactions regularly and do not open downloads that are attached to emails, from recipients that consumers are unsure of. The Federal Tarde Commission also lists steps that a consumer can take to report these types of phishing scams. A consumer can file a report directly with the Federal Trade Commission through the FTC’s website, or thorough and email that the FTC has set up specifically for reporting phishing scams. First responders, such as law enforcement officials, are also able to use the Anti-Phishing Working Group. “The Anti-Phishing Working Group, a group of ISPs, security vendors, financial institutions and law enforcement agencies, uses these reports to fight phishing." (FTC, 2006).

Ebay, one of the world's largest auctions sites, also has protections set up for consumers, as well as sellers who list items for sale within the Ebay website. The main thing that Ebay does to protect a consumer, is to offer a money back guarantee. The money back guarantee offered by Ebay covers items that a buyer does not receive, or items that arrive to the consumer that are not as described in the Ebay listing.

Items that a consumer purchases on Ebay, Ebay has a timeline that a consumer must abide by in order to qualify for Ebay's money back guarantee. "A buyer can report in My eBay that they didn't receive an item once the item's latest estimated delivery date has passed, and for 30 days after the latest estimated delivery date." (Ebay, 2015). For items that a consumer receives but are different than the item that is listed in the auction, the same timeline applies to the consumer.

For a consumer to submit a claim on Ebay, the consumer must first contact the seller to attempt to resolve the issue first. If the consumer cannot resolve the issue with the seller, the consumer may then start a ticket with Ebay, regarding the dispute. Ebay then goes in to review the transaction. If Ebay feels as though the consumer has been defrauded, Ebay will issue a refund directly to the consumer. The money back guarantee that Ebay offers is issued via PayPal to the consumer.

Other than protection to buyers, and sellers, Ebay also lists a warning on their website. The warning is regarding phishing scams. On EBay's website, Ebay warns consumers about phishing scams. Ebay has a page dedicated to informing consumers about email phishing scams. On this page, Ebay makes it clear that they "won't ask you to provide confidential information by email." (Ebay, 2015). Many of the tips Ebay gives to consumers, are the same tips provided to consumers by the Federal Trade Commission as well.

Consumers need to be aware of scams on the internet. One of the most important things to remember is to never share confidential information through email, and if the email looks suspicious, do not open it. Phishing is a common problem on the internet, and these are some precautionary steps a consumer can take to protect against email phishing scams. When dealing with online auction sites, such as Ebay, it is also imperative to read the steps they offer to buyers for protection from fraud as well.

References:

Ahmed, N. (2015). Extremist Right Wing Terrorist Groups | TRAC. Retrieved from https://www.trackingterrorism.org/article/extremist-right-wing-terrorist-groups

Al-Yazji, S. (2014, June 6). *GAZA LECTURER SUBHI AL-YAZJI: SUICIDE BOMBERS ARE MOTIVATED BY ISLAMIC FAITH, NOT FINANCIAL NEED OR BRAINWASHING*. Retrieved from https://www.memri.org/tv/gaza-lecturer-subhi-al-yazji-suicide-bombers-are-motivated-islamic-faith-not-financial-need-or

American Bar Association. (2015). State Policy Implementation Project - Pretrial Release. Retrieved from https://www.americanbar.org/content/dam/aba/admi

nistrative/criminal_justice/spip_pretrialrelease.authcheckdam.pdf

Anti-Defamation League. (2013). Aryan Brotherhood of Texas. Retrieved from https://www.adl.org/resources/profiles/aryan-brotherhood-of-texas

Associated Press. (2017, October 22). ARYAN BROTHERHOOD OF TEXAS. Retrieved from http://www.prisonoffenders.com/aryan_brotherhood_arrest_texas.html

Auge, K. (1999, October 14). No Indictment: Evidence voluminous but tricky. Retrieved from http://extras.denverpost.com/news/ram1014k.htm

Austin, J., Chan, L., & Elms, W. (1993). *Indiana Department Of Corrections Women Classification Study*. National Council On Crime and Deliquency.

Backes, D. (2012, August 15). A Look Back on 11 Years of Juvenile Justice Reform | Reclaiming Futures. Retrieved from https://www.reclaimingfutures.org/news/look-back-11-years-juvenile-justice-reform

Baradaran, S., Findley, M., Nielson, D., & Sharman, J. (2014). Funding Terror. *UNIVERSITY of PENNSYLVANIA LAW REVIEW*, *162*(3), 477-536.

Barnhart, T. (2009, November 9). Tell It Like It Is » Hot Tip - "Gangster Disciple". Retrieved from http://www.corrections.com/tracy_barnhart/?p=486

Berger, J. M. (2014, June 11). Domestic Terrorism Task Force 'More Than Overdue,' Experts Say. Retrieved from https://www.nbcnews.com/news/us-news/domestic-terrorism-task-force-more-overdue-experts-say-n128541

Briggs, S. (2009). *Criminology For Dummies.*

California Department of Corrections and Rehabilitation. (n.d.). The Rehabilitative Process. Retrieved from https://www.cdcr.ca.gov/Rehabilitation/Process.html

Chambliss, W. J. (2011). *Corrections.* Thousand Oaks: SAGE Publications.

Champion, D. J. (2011). *Sentencing: A reference handbook.* Santa Barbara, CA: ABC-CLIO.

CNN Library. (2017, December 12). ISIS Fast Facts. Retrieved from https://www.cnn.com/2014/08/08/world/isis-fast-facts/index.html

Connolly, S. (2013, February 26). 10 Most Dangerous Prison Gangs in the World. Retrieved from https://www.criminaljusticedegreehub.com/most-dangerous-prison-gangs/

Crime Museum LLC. (2015). Origins Of The Term Terrorism. Retrieved from https://www.crimemuseum.org/crime-library/terrorism/origins-of-the-term-terrorism/

Crime Scene Museum LLC. (2014). JonBenét Ramsey. Retrieved from https://www.crimemuseum.org/crime-library/cold-cases/jonbenet-ramsey/

Crossman, A. (2011). What Is Conflict Theory? Retrieved from http://sociology.about.com/od/Sociological-Theory/a/Conflict-Theory.htm

Del Cid Gómez, J. M. (n.d.). A Financial Profile of the Terrorism of Al-Qaeda and its Affiliates. *Perspectives on Terrorism, 04*(04), 3-27.

Delattre, E. J. (2011). *Character and cops: Ethics in policing* (6th ed.). Washington, DC: AEI Press.

Digital History - University of Houston. (2014). Terrorism in Historical Perspective. Retrieved from http://www.digitalhistory.uh.edu/topic_display.cfm?tcid=94

Eck, J. E., & Spelman, W. (1987). Problem-Oriented Policing. *National Institute of Justice - Research in Brief*, 1-7.

Fagan, P. (1995). *The Real Root Causes of Violent Crime: The Breakdown of Marriage, Family, and Community* . The Heritage Foundation.

Federal Bureau of Investigation. (2008, January 14). MS-13 Threat Assessment. Retrieved from https://archives.fbi.gov/archives/news/stories/2008/january/ms13_011408

Ferranti, S. (2015, May 15). Inside the History of the Black Guerrilla Family.

Financial Action Task Force: Groupe d'action financière. (2008). Terrorist financing.

FindLaw. (2014). Cruel and Unusual Punishment. Retrieved from https://criminal.findlaw.com/criminal-rights/cruel-and-unusual-punishment.html

Florida Department of Corrections. (2015). People and Folk Nation Sets -- Gang and Security Threat Group Awareness. Retrieved from http://www.dc.state.fl.us/pub/gangs/sets.html

Gauvin, J. (2015). *Lecture*.

Gill, C. (2014). Community-oriented policing to reduce crime, disorder and fear and increase satisfaction and legitimacy among citizens: a systematic review. *Journal of Experimental Criminology*, *10*(4), 399-428. doi:10.1007/s11292-014-9210-y

Greenblatt, A. (2014, August 4). Justice Department Finds Excessive Use Of Force At New York Prison. Retrieved from https://www.npr.org/sections/thetwo-way/2014/08/04/337850672/justice-department-finds-excessive-use-of-force-at-new-york-prison

Greenhouse, L. (2005, June 28). Justices Rule Police Do Not Have a Constitutional Duty to Protect Someone. Retrieved from https://www.nytimes.com/2005/06/28/politics/justices-rule-police-do-not-have-a-constitutional-duty-to-protect.html

Hames, J. B., & Akern, Y. (2015). *Introduction to law*. NJ: Pearson Education INC.

Helfgott, J. B. (2008). *Criminal Behavior: Theories, Typologies and Criminal Justice*. Sage Publications.

Hohenburg, J. (1935). The Lindbergh Kidnapping Trial. Retrieved from http://centennial.journalism.columbia.edu/1935-the-lindbergh-kidnapping-trial/index.html

Hutchinson, V. A., Keller, K., & Reid, T. (2009). *Inmate behavior management: The key to a safe and secure jail*. Washington, DC: U.S. Dept. of Justice, National Institute of Corrections.

Ibáñez, L. D. (2007). Suicide Terrorism Explained: A Psychosocial Approach. *Understanding Suicide Terrorism: Psychosocial Dynamics*, 18-41. doi:10.4135/9789351507901.n2

Izadi, E. (2016, April 29). Mom convicted for Facebook post about school-shooting rumor. Retrieved from https://www.washingtonpost.com/news/education/w

p/2016/04/29/mom-convicted-for-facebook-post-about-school-shooting-rumor/

Kim. (2006, May 16). Founder of MS-13 gang killed; had renounced violence. Retrieved from http://professorkim.blogspot.com/2006/05/founder-of-ms-13-gang-killed-had.html

Knox, G. (2004). GANG THREAT ANALYSIS: The Black Disciples. Retrieved from https://ngcrc.com/bdprofile.html

Kretchmar, J. (2008). Social Learning Theory.

Lanier, M. M., Briggs, L. T., & Oxford University Press. (2014). *Research methods in criminal justice and criminology: A mixed methods approach*. Oxford: Oxford University Press.

Leiner, B. M., Serf, V. G., & Clark, D. D. (1995). *A Brief History of the Internet*. Reston, VA: Internet Society.

Levine, N. (2002). *CrimeStat: A Spatial Statistics Program for the Analysis of Crime Incident Locations, version 2.0*. National Institute of Justice.

Lukens, R. J. (1999). *A critical handbook of children's literature*. New York, NY: Longman.

Luthern, A. (2016, May 9). Hales Corners man ruled incompetent for trial in mother's killing. Retrieved from www.jsonline.com/news/crime/hales-corners-man-ruled-incompetent-for-trial-in-mothers-killing-b99722082z1-378689841.html

Mason, E. (2015). The 'born criminal?? Lombroso and the origins of modern criminology. Retrieved from http://www.historyextra.com/article/feature/born-criminal-lombroso-origins-modern-criminology

Maswanganyi, M. (2016, June 18). #YouthDay: 'Youth day is not about drugs' ? Retrieved from http://www.news24.com/SouthAfrica/News/youthday-youth-day-is-not-about-drugs-mandla-maswanganyi-20160618

McGreal, C. (2017, December 5). Military given go-ahead to detain US terrorist suspects without trial. Retrieved from http://www.theguardian.com/world/2011/dec/15/americans-face-guantanamo-detention-obama

McLeod, S. (2008, February 5). Albert Bandura | Social Learning Theory | Simply Psychology. Retrieved from https://www.simplypsychology.org/bandura.html

McRae, L. (2013). Rehabilitating antisocial personalities: treatment through self-governance strategies. *The Journal of Forensic Psychiatry & Psychology*, *24*(1), 48-70. doi:10.1080/14789949.2012.752517

Mitchell, K. (2012, November 24). Man convicted of Fort Collins cold case released; now who killed Peggy Hettrick. Retrieved from http://blogs.denverpost.com/coldcases/2012/11/24/man-convicted-fort-collins-cold-case-released-killed-peggy-hettrick/5933/9/

Morales, G. (2013). Black Guerrilla Family. Retrieved from http://www.criminaljusticesolutionsham.org/black-guerrilla-family.html

O'Brien, M. (2014, October 18). Poor kids who do everything right don't do better than rich kids who do everything wrong. Retrieved from https://www.washingtonpost.com/news/wonk/wp/2014/10/18/poor-kids-who-do-everything-right-dont-do-better-than-rich-kids-who-do-everything-wrong/?utm_term=.f22e8f55c01e

O'Connor, T. (2015). Antisocial Personality, Sociopathy & Psychopathy.

OJJDP - Office of Juvenile Justice and Delinquency Program. (2010). *Community- and Problem-Oriented Policing*. Office of Juvenile Justice and Delinquency Program.

Osterburg, J. W., & Ward, R. H. (2014). *Criminal investigation: A method for reconstructing the past.* Cincinatti, OH: Anderson.

Possley, M. (2012, June). Timothy Masters - National Registry of Exonerations. Retrieved from http://www.law.umich.edu/special/exoneration/Pages/casedetail.aspx?caseid=3412

Reding, A., Gorp, A, Walczak, A., Giacomantonio, C., Hoorens, S., & RAND Europe. (2014). *Handling ethical problems in counterterrorism: An inventory of methods to support ethical decisionmaking*.

Reitan, E. (2010). Defining Terrorism for Public Policy Purposes: The Group-Target Definition. *Journal of Moral Philosophy*, 7(2), 253-278. doi:10.1163/174552409X12574076813513

Schmalleger, F. (2017). *Criminal justice today: An introductory text for the twenty-first century*(13th ed.).

Scott, M. (2000). *Problem-Oriented Policing: Reflections on the First 20 Years*. U.S. Department of Justice, Office of Community Oriented Policing Services.

Seymour, G. (2015). *Harry's game* (1st ed.). New York.

Siegel, L. J., & Bartollas, C. (2016). *Corrections today.* Belmont, CA: Wadsworth/Thomson Learning.

Skolnick, K. (2009). *A jailhouse lawyer's manual.* New York, NY: Columbia Human Rights Law Review.

Southern Poverty Law Center. (2015, November 1). Terror from the Right. Retrieved from https://www.splcenter.org/20151101/terror-right

Stohr, M. K., & Walsh, A. (2019). *Corrections: The essentials.*

U.S. Department of Justice. (2012). *Community Policing Defined.* Washington D.C.: Office of Community Oriented Policing Services.

U.S. Dept. of Justice. (2010). *Best practices to address community gang problems : OJJDP's Comprehensive Gang Model.* Retrieved from U.S.

Dept. of Justice, Office of Justice Programs, Office of Juvenile Justice and Delinquency Prevention website: https://www.ncjrs.gov/pdffiles1/ojjdp/231200.pdf

U.S. Dept. of Treasury. (2015). *National Terrorist Financing Risk Assessment*. Author.

Valdemar, R. (2007, July 25). History of the Mexican Mafia Prison Gang. Retrieved from http://www.policemag.com/blog/gangs/story/2007/07/history-of-the-mexican-mafia-prison-gang.aspx

Vincent. (2011). Community Policing vs. Problem Oriented Policing. Retrieved from http://gulfportpdchief.blogspot.com/2011/06/community-policing-vs-problem-oriented.html

Vogel, C., & Wilson, S. (2011, October 6). Cop's Book Says Sean Combs, Suge Knight Ordered Tupac and

Biggie Killings. Retrieved from http://www.laweekly.com/news/cops-book-says-sean-combs-suge-knight-ordered-tupac-and-biggie-killings-2172206

Weimann, G. (2004, March). How Modern Terrorism Uses the Internet. Retrieved from https://www.usip.org/sites/default/files/sr116.pdf

White, J. R. (2011). *Terrorism and homeland security.* Belmont, CA: Wadsworth Cengage Learning.

Yero, A., Othman, J., Abu Samah, B., D'Silva, J. L., & Sulaiman, A. H. (2012). Re-visiting concept and theories of community policing. *International Journal of Academic Research*, *4*(4), 51-55. doi:10.7813/2075-4124.2012/4-4/b.7

Zinn, B. (2016, October 20). Gang members operate behind bars. Retrieved from https://www.newsleader.com/story/news/local/2016/

10/20/gang-members-operate-behind-

bars/91657568/

www.ingramcontent.com/pod-product-compliance
Lightning Source LLC
Chambersburg PA
CBHW030759180526
45163CB00003B/1095

* 9 7 8 0 3 5 9 2 7 1 8 0 1 *